Beckett Great Sports Heroes

Shaquille O'Neal

By the staff of Beckett Publications

House of Collectibles • New York

Published by: House of Collectibles
201 East 50th Street
New York, NY 10022

Distributed by Ballantine Books, a division of Random House, Inc., New York,
and simultaneously in Canada by Random House of Canada Limited, Toronto.

Manufactured in the United States of America

ISBN: 0-876-37980-3

Cover design by Michaelis/Carpelis Design Associates

Cover photo by Barry Gossage/NBA Photos

First Edition: October 1995

10   9   8   7   6   5   4   3   2   1

Foreword

Forecast: Reign

As great as Shaquille O'Neal's first three years in the NBA have been, an even brighter future beckons

Shaq's future is as bright as his megawatt smile.

He entered the NBA by storm as a 20-year-old man-child. And now, almost three years later, the storm still rages.

Shaquille O'Neal is like one of those high-pressure weather patterns so familiar to Floridians — a bundle of energy that slowly, relentlessly gathers force until it wreaks havoc upon hitting land.

And understand, Shaq hasn't reached full force yet. Despite being a nearly unanimous pick for 1993 Rookie of the Year, finishing second in the league in scoring as a sophomore and leading Orlando to the NBA Finals last season, O'Neal's potential remains as boundless as his zest for life.

Sure, he's added shots and moves to his game, expanding his repertoire beyond thunderous slam dunks. And yes, he has worked on his free-throw shooting, the only apparent Achilles' heel on this near-mythic figure. But additional room for improvement remains. Thus, a sobering thought for the league's 28 other franchises: He will get better.

But what is ominous news for his opponents is a welcome forecast for his fans. Shaq is one storm they can eagerly anticipate.

Gary Santaniello
Gary Santaniello
Senior Editor

CONTENTS

He's a marketing

phenomenon, a budding

entrepreneur and an

increasingly mature and

potent force on the

basketball court. Every-

thing that Shaquille O'Neal

desires is well within

his grasp.

The World Is His

By Barry Cooper

Orlando Magic general manager Pat Williams, famous for his one-liners, used to quip that star center Shaquille O'Neal is so wealthy his wallet qualifies as carry-on baggage. But now, no wallet can contain all of Shaq's riches.

Three years ago during his rookie season, Shaq removed some pocket change in front of a wide-eyed television reporter. Out came a wad of bills as thick as an encyclopedia. Shaq, holding about $7,000 in $100 bills, grinned sheepishly at the camera.

If Shaq was toting around $7,000 as a rookie, what's he packing now? Ten grand? Fifty?

Shaq isn't telling. He's a lot richer than he was three seasons ago, and much more private, too. No TV reporter is going to film him counting his money. And if Shaq can help it, no one will know the details of his endorsement contracts.

Some players enter the NBA hoping to become the next Wilt Chamberlain, Julius Erving or Larry Bird. Like a lot of other young players, Shaq thinks about that, too. But he thinks even more about becoming the next Donald Trump, Ted Turner or Bill Gates.

When he lies awake at night, Shaq, 23, thinks about the accomplishments of those people.

"I want to be an entrepreneur, a very successful one," he says. "Basketball? I know I can play basketball. I've always been good at that, and I want to be one of the best ever to play the game. But when I retire, I also want to have my own businesses."

Aspiring to become rich and famous outside sports illustrates Shaq's maturation. As O'Neal looks ahead to his fourth NBA season, his agent, Leonard Armato, continues to skillfully guide his career.

SCOTT CUNNINGHAM / NBA PHOTOS

After promoting Shaq to the point of overexposure his rookie campaign, Armato backed off in seasons two and three, carefully picking his spots. As the 1995 NBA playoffs began, Armato negotiated a contract for Shaq to star in two movies the next two years, one as a genie in an action comedy, another as a Bruce Lee-style karate star in another.

B-grade movies? Maybe. But, according to sources, Armato and O'Neal will have total control over his participation in the films. It's all part of Armato's crafty handling of O'Neal, the hottest young player in sports.

The agent has made Shaq a $16 million-a-year man, based on a $4.8 million salary from the Magic, a $3 million-a-year endorsement deal with Pepsi and a multiyear deal with Reebok reportedly worth more than $25 million. A beaming Armato told Newsweek that the mega contracts represent only the tip of a very large iceberg for Shaq.

Michael Jordan, with an estimated income of $30 million a year in endorsements, remains the king of the ad game. But his heir apparent is obvious: Shaq.

"It's like Jordan was the best stereo ever, and along comes Shaq and he's digital," Armato told Newsweek.

Armato continues to market Shaq like some hot, high-tech product. O'Neal's first film, Blue Chips, wasn't a hit, and that sent Armato scurrying to study the success of actors such as Sylvester Stallone. Sly isn't a great actor, yet his movies rake in millions. Shaq's going to copy the formula by appearing in films as a superhero — an easy sell to impressionable

young teens. How 'bout Rambo and Shaq take on aliens from Mars?

Armato also is talking about Shaq starting his own record label, and even venturing into cyberspace with something that would be called Shaq On-line.

How many home computer buffs would want to go one-on-one with Shaq? Thousands? Millions? How many advertisers would rush to grab a piece of the action, forking over hundreds of thousands of dollars for the privilege? Shaq could become one of the biggest attractions on the Internet.

Can you blame him for sporting a tattoo that pictures the globe grasped by a large hand, accompanied by the words "The World Is Mine"?

His fan club already boasts 60,000 members, and with the Magic likely to contend for the championship the next 10 years or so, that number could grow tenfold or more.

But Shaq's smart enough to know the hottest celebrities in sports play on teams that last deep into the playoffs. Jordan racked up invaluable television exposure by driving the Bulls to three consecutive world championships. The world loves a winner, and Shaq knows the more he wins, the more people will embrace him — and buy his products.

In addition to his acting and business deals, he's also a budding rapper with two hit albums. He always has something to sell, and in sales, exposure is everything.

"I said early in the season that my goal is to play until June," Shaq said, referring, of course, to the NBA Finals. "I know people who measure my skills will measure me by whether or not I win a championship. I look at Patrick Ewing; he has never won a championship. That has to be something that bothers you."

The Magic love hearing their young star talk like that. It's another part of his maturation.

Shaq symbolically supplanted Michael Jordan as the NBA's ascendant player when the Magic eliminated Chicago in the Eastern Conference semifinals.

The lone chink in O'Neal's armor is his free-throw shooting, but Shaq always has been an eager student when it comes to improving any facet of his game.

He came to the team as a big, lovable kid with enormous raw basketball talent and strength. Three years later, he has refined his skills, improved his offensive game and — more importantly — has become a true team leader and a consummate professional.

With Jordan's skills having eroded some despite his much-ballyhooed comeback, O'Neal realizes more than ever he's the biggest, most visible attraction in basketball. When Orlando beat Chicago, 4-2, in its best-of-seven Eastern Conference semifinal series, it meant more than merely a berth in the Eastern Conference finals. It signaled a passing of the torch. The young, upstart Magic stripped Jordan and the Bulls of the great aura of invincibility they once enjoyed. And by leading his team to victory, Shaq showed everyone that he is The Man now — not Jordan.

"He's done everything we've asked of him — and more," says John Gabriel, the Magic's vice president for basketball operations/player personnel. "What some people don't realize is how hard Shaq works. When you look at him, you're looking at a mature young man who wants to be as good as he can be. He wants to make the players around him better. He wants to win championships. You don't always see those elements in players, especially young players. And it's really special when you see it in a player who is as gifted as Shaq is."

Around the league, veteran basketball observers continue to rave about Shaq.

"We've got no answer for him,"

ANDREW BERNSTEIN / NBA PHOTOS

says Boston Celtics vice president M.L. Carr. "It's impossible to match up against Orlando because very few teams in the league can match up against Shaq. I have to admit, though, he's a good kid, and he's good for the league. He's very likable."

Shaq's winsome personality is in

high gear when he meets with kids or performs charity work. Some cynics rolled their eyes at Shaq's public service work as a rookie, figuring Armato was using the opportunities as publicity stunts. They were wrong. Three years later, Shaq still meets with disadvantaged children before games, treating the

homeless to free Thanksgiving dinners and spending up to $50,000 each Christmas on toys for deserving children.

That doesn't mean O'Neal always is perfect. Open and engaging during his rookie year, he's sometimes more temperamental now — like many other celebrities settling into superstardom. On the second long day of filming for a Pepsi commercial, Shaq grew more and more irritated. It takes hours and hours to get a commercial just right, and when the crew announced it was breaking for lunch, Shaq shook his head from side to side. He said he'd leave for the day and go home if the crew stopped.

After much discussion the crew members shrugged their shoulders and went back to work, only to see Shaq, clearly weary, abruptly call a halt to the proceedings three hours later. They couldn't coax Shaq into staying around for the final photo session of the day.

The incident illustrates how Shaq sometimes is affected by the intense demands on his time. Somebody always is tugging at his elbow. The questions come at him like fastballs from Nolan Ryan. Sign this, Shaq. Look here, Shaq. Come here, Shaq.

His personal assistant, Dennis Tracey, tries without much success to shield O'Neal from an adoring public. Folks have been known to appear at the guarded entrance leading to Shaq's 22,000-square foot mansion, insisting they have an appointment. He constantly has to change his phone number. Everybody wants to see The House.

There are 16 rooms and nine bathrooms in the place. Reportedly, Shaq's bedroom covers 2,500 square feet — bigger than many houses. Precious few reporters have been invited inside. Those who have, marvel at Shaq's graciousness. He's also becoming a consummate gen-tleman. Have a seat on Shaq's couch and not long afterward, Shaq's personal cook will appear, offering to bake home-made cookies or whip up a special meal or snack.

Everybody who visits comes away wowed.

Presumably, there have been female guests, but Shaq won't talk about girl-friends. And none apparently talk publicly about him. The tabloids have been trying for years to uncover his romances — with no success. Amazingly, the man actually keeps his private life private.

That's fine with the Magic. They have exactly what they want: an improving superstar who's becoming a total professional on and off the court.

As a pitchman for many products, Shaq sometimes is burdened by the obligations, but at his palatial home in Orlando he's dogged by no one.

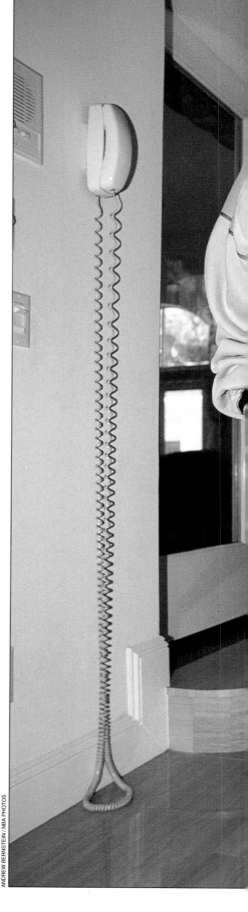

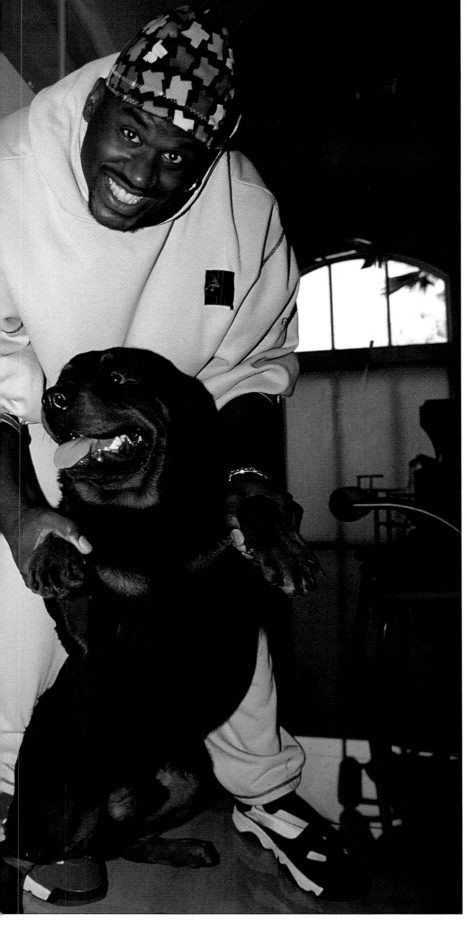

ike Jordan and other stars, Shaq has learned to steer clear of potentially explosive social issues. But he did raise some eyebrows with his autobiographical rap song, "Biological Didn't Bother," in which he rejects overtures from his birth father, who abandoned him when he was a baby. The song is dedicated to his stepfather, Philip Harrison, a retired army sergeant who married Shaq's mom, Lucille, when Shaq was two.

"Phil's my father because my biological didn't bother," Shaq raps. If only briefly, the song raised the country's awareness of the importance of fatherhood and responsibility. When Shaq speaks — or raps — people do listen.

"Take a good look at him," says forward Dennis Scott, Shaq's closest friend on the team. "Because when he's gone, you'll never see another like him."

The Magic don't like to even think about the day O'Neal will move on. Obviously, retirement is far away, but would Shaq say, consider a jump to the Los Angeles Lakers or New York Knicks via free agency? Think about it. A major media market such as the Big Apple or L.A. would only enhance Shaq's incredible marketing power.

But O'Neal surrenders fewer secrets than a master poker player. "I have to keep you all guessing," he says.

Shaq reportedly can become a restricted free agent after next season. That would open the door to his becoming an unrestricted free agent the next season. No one expects that to happen, though. The Magic are expected to offer him a contract worth more than $100 million.

That ought to provide the sports world's most visible player with enough pocket change to make it through, oh, another week or so.   •

Barry Cooper is a columnist for The Orlando Sentinel.

Shaq's larger-than-life impact on and off the court has made this 'Little Warrior' a household name

sizable
differences

give
him a
hand

Palm a basketball? This hand could palm a Hyundai.
But if you think that's something, turn the page and check
out what happens when Shaq puts his best foot forward.

ucille O'Neal-Harrison wanted to give her children unique names, the kind people would remember.

On March 6, 1972, Shaquille Rashaun O'Neal, all 7 pounds, 11 ounces of him, was introduced to the world. In Islamic tradition, Shaquille Rashaun means "Little Warrior."

"To me, just having a name that means something makes you special," she says.

Shaquille isn't the only unique name in the Harrison clan. Ayesha and Lateefah, his sisters, and Jamal, his brother, also were given special names.

The Harrisons decided to make Shaquille's last name O'Neal — Lucille's maiden name — in order to keep her family name going.

Today, the Little Warrior has become one of the world's biggest names. Shaquille — a.k.a. Shaq — has made his mother proud. Not only has his name become part of every basketball fan's vocabulary, but it has matched — if not surpassed — its original meaning.

Still, "Little" and Shaq never have fit together appropriately.

As a junior high student, Shaq already stood at the top of his class — literally. At 6-4, he was two inches taller than his mother and creeping in on his father's 6-7 height. Philip Harrison knew someday soon he'd be looking up at his son.

Before Shaq's junior year in high school, that day arrived. He stood at 6-8. Basketball coaches were awestruck over this Goliath's mere presence in the halls. But where most boys this tall, this dominating in the paint, might see themselves as another

how do you
measure up?

Wilt Chamber-
lain, Bill Russell or
Kareem Abdul-Jabbar, Shaq idol-
ized Julius Erving, the silky smooth doctor of dunk.

Ironically, even at 6-8, Shaq had trouble getting his first dunk. "I just couldn't do it for a long time. It was frustrating," O'Neal remembers. "Then, finally, one day it just happened. It was a real weak dunk, but it was a dunk."

Basketball rims and backboards around the country haven't been the same since.

It's uncertain whether Shaq finally has stopped growing. He currently stands at **7-1, 303** pounds. His shirt size is **52**, his waist measures **46** inches. His shoes are **22 EEE**. And his hands . . . well, let's just say he's never had a problem palming a basketball. In fact, the ball looks like a grape-fruit when Shaq wraps his hand around it.

Despite these Frankenstein-like dimensions, Shaq still moves, on and off the court, like Dr. J. When Shaq's not exploding past defenseless centers, he's bustin' a move on the dance floor. About the only thing he likes as much as a nasty, back-board-obliterating dunk is his rap music. It might seem impossible for a human this big to be light on his feet, but then again, Shaq has been special from Day One. His mother made sure of it.   •

Shaquille
O'Neal
brought
down
the
house in
more
ways
than
anyone
ever

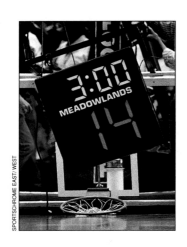

could
have
imagined
in his
break-out
rookie
season

**By Barry
Cooper**

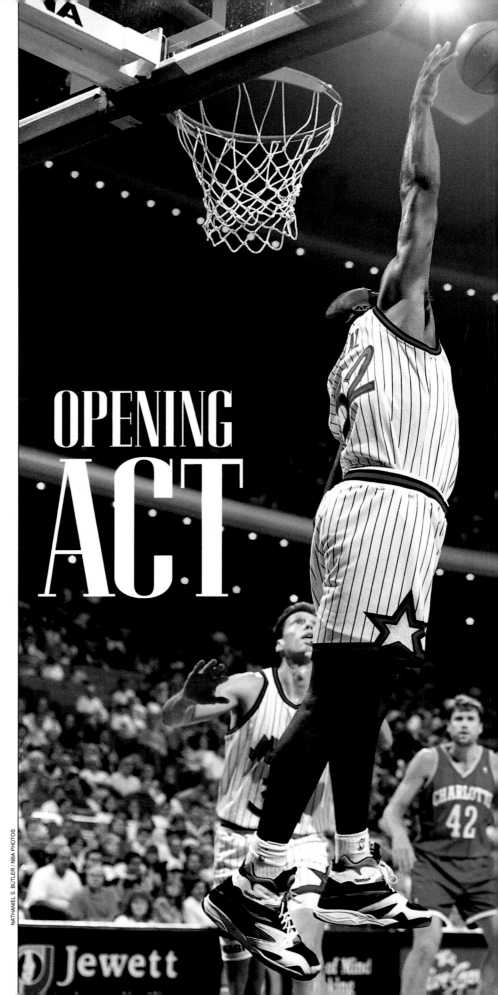

OPENING
ACT

LIGHTS, CAMERA, ACTION

**Shaq's first NBA game
November 6, 1992**

Orlando Magic 110

Miami Heat 100

SHAQUILLE O'NEAL

32 minutes

4-8 fgm-fga

4-7 ftm-fta

18 rebounds

2 assists

6 fouls

12 points

Flashback to October 1992: Shaquille O'Neal, wearing combat boots and a shirt missing sleeves, boards the bus for his first NBA training camp. The Magic are training at Stetson University in nearby DeLand, Fla., but O'Neal looks more like a gung ho recruit headed for boot camp at Parris Island.

Instead of taking his lumps from the NBA's toughest drill sergeants, however, this rookie made it perfectly clear that he would be the one administering the punishment.

season, O'Neal ripped down a defensive rebound, dribbled the length of the floor and jammed at the other end.

Never has a city or league been so captivated by a kid who wasn't old enough even to buy a beer.

NBA fans quickly learned never to say never when talking about Shaq.

Greg Kite, a veteran big man assigned to work against this man-child during camp, was the first NBA player to be formally introduced to the Shaq Attack.

Taking the ball in the low post, Shaq dribbled a few times and slammed

less times during the '92-93 campaign. Fortunately for Kite, he watched most of these episodes from the safety of the Magic bench.

Comparisons to legendary big man Wilt Chamberlain began the instant commissioner David Stern called Shaq's name first at the 1992 NBA draft. For the next 82 games, O'Neal made a convincing case for reaching — maybe even surpassing — such lofty expectations.

He was the season's first Player of the Week, the first time a rookie ever had won the award at the start of the season. He tore down backboards in

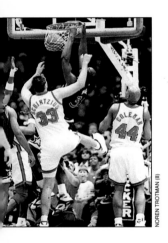

NOREN TROTMAN (8)

Shaq adopted one basic philosophy from his first day as a pro: Take no prisoners.

Never has there been a rookie in any sport quite like Shaq.

Never has there been an athlete this big (7-1, 303 pounds) who's this quick and this stylish. More than once during his debut

hard into Kite like an automobile driver mistakenly taking off in reverse. Kite's grunt echoed throughout the gym, but the referees working this scrimmage looked on blankly, their silent whistles dangling from their lips.

Somehow, Kite stood his ground. O'Neal backed into him again, causing another violent collision. This one could have upended a minivan. Kite lost his footing and fell to the floor. O'Neal, his path finally clear, let out a scream as he slammed home a two-handed thunder dunk.

This scene was played out count-

Phoenix and New Jersey. He led Orlando in points (23.4), rebounds (13.9) and blocks (3.53), and was the runaway choice for Rookie of the Year.

O'Neal was a rarity. He actually exceeded his advanced hype.

Responding to Shaq's attacks, league officials hired a structural-design firm to test the bolts and screws of each basket in every NBA arena during the off-season to make sure they could withstand the force of O'Neal's most vicious jams.

"The guy attacks the basket like no one I've ever seen," former star forward

Larry Nance says. "I want to see the guy who would even think of attempting to block one of his dunks. I guarantee that he'd break your hand if you tried it.

"In the [early season] game we played against them, I remember going up for a defensive rebound. I was sure I had the ball. All of a sudden, he's got it and went right back up for a dunk."

Nance was by no means the only player to have his eyes opened by the big guy.

"This kid reminds me of Mike Tyson when Tyson was Mike Tyson," guard John Battle explains. "He's mas-

ond only to the Chicago Bulls in road attendance Shaq's rookie season. And when Michael headed for the baseball diamond, O'Neal's traveling show moved to No. 1.

Like any true showman, Shaq always gives his audience its money's worth.

Under the bright lights of NBC's cameras, O'Neal caused a 37-minute delay when he tore down a goal standard in the NBA's newest facility, America West Arena in Phoenix. It was the first time the Magic ever had been

No post player in the league can shut him down. The only centers who present problems are San Antonio's David Robinson, Houston's Hakeem Olajuwon and Charlotte's Alonzo Mourning. All three possess the low-post agility and size necessary to challenge Shaq.

New York's Patrick Ewing also plays Shaq tough. Ewing's physical presence and veteran savvy put Shaq to the test. But O'Neal passed this exam with flying colors during his debut season.

In four meetings with Ewing, Shaq averaged 21 points, 14.5 re-

sive. I'm a fight fan, and when Tyson fought, I know there were guys who lost on intimidation alone. [Shaq's] intimidating in the same way."

Intimidation may have cleared Shaq plenty of room in the paint, but his magical personality — on and off the court — made him a marquee attraction. As his agent Leonard Armato put it, "Shaq is a cross between the Terminator and Bambi."

O'Neal became a box-office hit at every stop. Orlando, a franchise previously suffering from an identity crisis since its inception in 1989, ranked sec-

featured in a nationally televised game. Phoenix won the game, 121-105, when O'Neal ran into foul trouble. But the next day, no one remembered the final score. The highlight of Shaq's earth-shaking slam ran for months. Not surprisingly, NBC scheduled Orlando to play on national television seven times in '93-94.

"I just go out and play my game," Shaq says. "I feel that I have the size, the strength and the skills to play in this league. It's just a matter of me going out and applying myself. I'm not 'The Man' in this league yet, but someday, I may be."

bounds and 4.75 blocks. Ewing's averages were 15 points, 13 boards and 2.25 blocks.

To top it off, Shaq became just the 14th rookie to start an All-Star Game — the first since Jordan in 1985 — when he outdistanced Ewing in the Eastern Conference voting. Shaq finished fourth overall in the balloting behind Jordan, Scottie Pippen and Charles Barkley.

In the game, O'Neal played 25 minutes, scored 14 points and diplomatically dodged some controversy afterward.

YOUTH IS SERVED

Shaquille O'Neal was 20 years old when he scored his first NBA point, threw his first NBA elbow and won his first NBA game. Here's a look at what other great NBA centers were up to when they were 20:

Wilt Chamberlain was beginning his sophomore season at the University of Kansas.

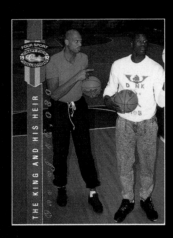

Bill Russell was finishing his second season at the University of San Francisco.

Bill Walton was starting his third season at UCLA.

Kareem Abdul-Jabbar was wrapping up his second season at UCLA.

Patrick Ewing was starting his second season at Georgetown.

Hakeem Olajuwon was a junior at the University of Houston.

"He is one of the most exciting players in the game as far as big men are concerned, but he has still got to get by [Hakeem] Olajuwon before he can be considered the best in the game right now. It's not fair to compare him with Wilt [Chamberlain] right now. Wilt is still the man." — Calvin Murphy, former Houston Rockets guard

"He palms the ball like a grapefruit. He's as big as Mark Eaton but 20 times as quick. give me a break!" — Rony Seikaly, Golden State Warriors Center

SHAQ RAP

"Shaq can do anything he wants to do. He's the man. Why worry about having an outside shot when you can dominate under the basket like he can?" — Isiah Thomas, former All-Star guard

"My compliments go out to the big fellow. He has got a great game, very nice. The most frightening thing about him is his size. It allows him to have his way around the basket." — Hakeem Olajuwan, Houston Rockets All-Star center

"Shaq is just a monster. With that great body he has, that great size, he can walk on the court and get 15 [points] and 10 [rebounds] without breaking a sweat. He's just a monster. We haven't seen anyone come into the league in a long time with that combination of skill and power. Who's going to stop that?" — Magic Johnson, future Hall of Famer

"Right now, I would say he is not a threat with his back-to-the-basket moves, but you have got to know where he is all the time. When he is in the flow, he is dangerous. If you're in at center against him, you have just got to concentrate on guarding him and not worry about helping out on anybody else." — Dave Cowens, Hall of Fame center

"He has incredible talent, but great success doesn't come easy in this league for anyone. He is going to have to keep working at it. He still needs a few more offensive moves besides his dunks, and his free-throw shooting obviously needs to be worked on. But there isn't any questioning of his skills. He has all the tools."
— Tom Heinsohn,
Hall of Fame forward

"He is a great player. He's very smart and very consistent. You didn't see him getting out of control like a lot of other rookies. He does just about everything he wants out there." — Bobby Jones, defensive wizard for the 76ers throughout the 1980s

"If I was guarding Shaq, I would hope that I was in great condition and weighed 450 pounds. because that is the kind of guy it is going to take to stop him."— Artis Gilmore, former center who starred in the ABA

AL MESSERSCHMIDT

"Once he really learns how to play the game, he is going to be the greatest player ever. Would I take a ball to the basket against him? Look, I took the ball to the hole against anybody. I took it to the hole against Wilt. But Shaq's a great player. All he needs is a couple of more shots." — Connie Hawkins, former ABA star

"If I was a coach, this is the one guy I would like to have on my team. In a few years, you probably are going to see him become one of the greatest centers ever to play in the NBA. The only way to defend that guy is to keep the ball out of his hands. Once he has got the ball, he's too big to do anything with." — Zelmo Beaty, former center for four NBA teams including the Lakers and the Jazz

"If he gets good position down low, forget it. He is so big and strong that nobody can stop him when he has got great position underneath. The only thing you can hope to do is try to push him out away from the basket a bit more and hope he misses."
— Chuck Daly, former head coach

Before writing his ow book during the off-s (Shaq Attaq!), Mr O' rewrote the Magic's book with a rookie se to remember. Here a of the records he nov

MAGIC SINGLE-SEASO RECORDS

1,893 points

286 blocks

.562 fg percentage

1,122 rebounds

733 fgm

321 personal fouls

8 disqualifications

23.4 scoring

721 fta

427 ftm

307 turnovers

ELITE FRATERNITY

Shaquille O'Neal became just the 14th rookie starter in the 43-year history of the All-Star Game. Here's the company he joins:

SHAQUILLE O'NEAL

Bob Cousy
Ray Felix
Tom Heinsohn
*Wilt Chamberlain
*Oscar Robertson
Walt Bellamy
Jerry Lucas
Luke Jackson
Rick Barry
Elvin Hayes
Magic Johnson
Isiah Thomas
Michael Jordan

*Voted the game's MVP

Asked if he was upset about his limited playing time — Eastern Conference head coach Pat Riley, who coaches Ewing in New York, sat the rookie down for a 16-minute stretch — Shaq said he was just glad to be out there having fun.

Good Answer.

The Magic seem destined to win more than they lose with their blossoming legend in the lineup.

When critics said Shaq would run into "The Wall," the invisible barrier all rookies succumb to after their first 50 or so games, Shaq blasted through it. He finished the season as strong as he started it. The year before O'Neal arrived, the Magic were 21-61. In Shaq's debut season, they finished 41-41 and barely missed the playoffs.

"I have always imagined myself a few pounds heavier and a couple of inches taller," says the Rockets' Olajuwon. "I think now I know what I would look like. He reminds me of me."

Olajuwon has become the most skillful center in the league, and O'Neal looks up to him because of that. They even share the same agent in Armato. O'Neal also would like to follow Hakeem's footsteps into the winner's circle. Claiming a championship, as Olajuwon did with the Rockets, ranks at the top of Shaq's want list.

Shaq knows he must win it all to be considered the best.

Chamberlain, who needed eight seasons to claim his first world title, knows the type of pressure that will fall on Shaq's shoulders if a championship doesn't arrive in Disney World soon. But Wilt grows tired of the constant comparisons between his game and Shaq's.

"I see Shaquille as a man totally playing his own game of basketball," Chamberlain says. "The bottom line for me is I'd love to see him given the chance to play basketball with his own athletic ability and style, let him be Shaquille O'Neal and not the new Wilt Chamberlain, or anyone else.

"I had the pleasure to film a commercial with Shaquille, Bill Russell, Bill Walton and Kareem. I was thoroughly impressed with Shaquille as a young man. I thought he had a lot of class, style and a lot of enthusiasm."

Shaq grins when asked about his brush with Wilt.

"I want to be me," Shaq says. "I want to have my own style, my own way of playing. People can say anything about me that they want. Like I said, I'll never knock a man for his opinion."

O'Neal realizes his statistics speak for themselves. In just 34 games, he established a Magic record for blocked shots. He racked up at least 20 points in 50 games. He scored 30 or more points 10 times. And it was only the beginning. Basic training was over in a flash, and Shaq already promoted himself. But not just any promotion would do. As always, Shaq was thinking big. He arrived for training camp for his second season sporting a tattoo of the Superman logo on his right bicep.

Up, up, and away. •

Barry Cooper is a columnist for The Orlando Sentinel.

ROCKY WIDNER

About the only thing that didn't go smoothly for Shaquille during his rookie season was that his college jersey No. 33 wasn't available.

ANDREW D. BERNSTEIN / NBA PHOTOS

ACT II

After an off-season filled with movies, concerts and bad press, Shaq finally concentrated on basketball and turned in a marvelous sophomore performance

By Bill Fay

Shaquille O'Neal may have shown up for Act II with a Superman tattoo on one arm and the league's Rookie of the Year hardware under the other, but something else not so glowing also arrived with him.

"Shaq-bashing is in," he said ruefully after inspecting a few samples of the negative stories written about him during the off-season.

Shaq-bashing definitely was all the rage in Orlando and around the NBA. While the preseason should have been fueled by expectations for the new union of Shaq and Penny Hardaway, whom the Magic acquired on draft day 1993, it instead was filled with gossip columns about O'Neal's summer vacation and how it would hinder his development as the superstar of the '90s.

It can't be denied. Shaq's off-season was, to put it mildly, busy.

• First, there was the movie, a feature film about college basketball called *Blue Chips*. O'Neal shared top billing with Nick Nolte. But the relationship Shaq built with Hardaway, who along with O'Neal played one of the recruits, proved most rewarding for the Magic.

• Then came the book, an autobiography with *Sports Illustrated* writer Jack McCallum that offered personal insights into Shaq's childhood and his rookie season in the NBA.

Shaq's sophomore season, which ended with an ignominious three-game sweep at the hands of the Pacers in the first round of the playoffs, left him determined to improve.

• A rap single ("What's Up Doc") followed, and shortly afterwards his first solo album *(Shaq Diesel)* hit the shelves. It since has gone platinum.

• He toured the Orient and parts of Western Europe on behalf of Reebok.

Those were his working hour activities. What the press in those ports didn't see, or failed to report, was the time Shaq spent working on his game.

O'Neal hired a tutor to teach him kung fu in an effort to improve his foot and hand speed. He spent a week at the renowned Pete Newell Big Man Camp in Hawaii, where he was judged "the hardest worker in my camp" by the demanding Newell.

"I always made time to work on my game," O'Neal said of his off-season regimen. "I had a trainer with me everywhere, and we'd work out together, shooting, running, playing games. I paid attention to my real job, which is basketball. It's just that people were paying more attention to the other stuff I was doing."

The critics certainly were. Shaq was all hype and glitter with no game, they said. He's taking free trips when he ought to be improving his free throws. His focus always will be on selling himself instead of winning championships, they sniped.

"Jealousy. That's all it is right there, jealousy," O'Neal answered.

From the opening tip of his second season, Shaq was on a mission to prove them wrong. He broke from the blocks with 42, 36 and 37 points in his first three games, all Magic victories.

"I think what you get with

O'Neal experienced few explosive moments at the All-Star Game, where he was shackled by a pointedly suffocating West defense.

Shaquille is a guy who is motivated by challenges, and all the criticism he took about his summer really motivated him to come out strong," Magic head coach Brian Hill said. "I don't expect him to sustain this pace all season, but I think he's sent a clear message that he did more last summer than just stand in front of a camera and smile."

O'Neal did back off the torrid scoring pace, but still finished as the top scorer the first half of the season. The fans responded by voting him the starting center in the All-Star Game for the second year in a row. In fact, Shaq was the leading vote getter in the Eastern Conference, a testimony to his popularity with the people, if not with the press.

But all was not as perfect as it seemed. All-Star Weekend should have been a Shaq celebration. Instead, it became another Shaq bash.

O'Neal, as he likes to do, jammed his calendar with appearances and promotions.

"There are 24 hours in a day," he said. "If I spend two or three of them on basketball, that gives me 21 to fill. I only need about four or five hours of sleep a night, so I'm left with 16 hours. What am I supposed to do with them? Sit around in my room and watch TV? I'm not that kind of guy. I like to get out and do things. I'm young, I've got energy and I've got talents. Let me use them."

His concert and TV appearances were criticized heavily as were his promotional tie-ins. But that was nothing compared to what happened in the game itself.

The first time O'Neal touched the ball, he was surrounded by three players from the West. Next time he caught it, four players boxed him so tightly he was called for traveling just trying to get

out. In fact, the double- and triple-teaming continued the entire game. The West All-Stars effectively put O'Neal in a telephone booth and challenged him to emerge as Superman.

"We were just doing what the coach asked us to," Utah's Karl Malone said, flashing a mischievous smile.

O'Neal missed all eight shots he took in the first half. He finished the game with eight points. His backup for the game, New York's Patrick Ewing, scored 20 points and didn't face a double-team the whole evening.

O'Neal recognized that a conspiracy had been played out against him, but he

> **We'll be back. I'm going home to work on my own — no movies, no rap concerts, lots of basketball. You're going to see a much better player next fall.**
> — Shaquille O'Neal

refused to criticize his opponents. He spent 20 minutes telling reporters that "all that double- and triple-teaming just means they respect me," but as he walked out of the locker room, he turned to a small group of writers he knew and said: "Somebody is going to pay for this."

As fate would have it, the Magic's second opponent after the All-Star Game was the Seattle SuperSonics. The Sonics were coached by George Karl, the same guy who coached the West All-Star team. Karl paid in full.

O'Neal scored 38 points and grabbed 20 rebounds in slightly more than three quarters of play as the Magic routed Seattle, 124-93. "I wanted to mutilate them, destroy them and humiliate them," O'Neal said.

O'Neal continued to lead the league in scoring, and the Magic kept

their pace toward a 50-win season as the regular season drew to a close. In fact, on the final night, O'Neal led David Robinson by a few tenths of a point in scoring, and the Magic had 49 victories. Both birds could be killed with the same stone.

As the Magic prepared to play New Jersey, however, word filtered in that Robinson was having a monster night against the Los Angeles Clippers. He scored 71 points, meaning O'Neal would need 68 to beat him out of the scoring title. Shaq scored just 32, but the Magic got the victory.

"It would have been nice to see Robinson get 40 or even 50 so I'd have something to shoot at, but the scoring title really wasn't the most important thing," O'Neal said. "The most important thing was for us to win 50 games. That's what is really important to the organization."

The Magic entered the playoffs as the No. 4 seed against Indiana, which was on a roll, having won its final eight regular season games. The Pacers rolled right over Orlando, sweeping the shocked Magic in three games.

"This is the most down I've ever felt," O'Neal said after averaging 20.7 points and shooting just 47.1 percent from the line in three playoff games. "I guess this just means we have to go home and work harder. That's the secret. You can't just show up and play and expect to get a championship.

"But we'll be back. I'm going home to work on my own — no movies, no rap concerts, lots of basketball. You're going to see a much better player next fall."

The rest of the league soon wished that Shaq hadn't taken defeat so seriously. •

Bill Fay covers the Magic for The Tampa Tribune.

Act III

Carrying the Magic to new heights as a force in the playoffs, Shaq quiets the critics who questioned his ability to succeed where it counts most

By Mark Emmons

As the "Shaq Does the NBA" Tour rolled into its third year in the fall of 1994, this is what we knew about the league's resident man-child:

He could score. Rebound. Block shots. Rap. Act. Sell lots of products.

Only one question hovered above Shaquille O'Neal's mountainous frame: Could he win?

Ah, that was the $64,000 question, which is probably just about what Shaq pulls down each game. And we're not, of course, just talking about winning 50-plus games in the regular season. That was a given. Shaq had been there, done that.

No, as the 1994-95 season was about to dawn, the high stakes confronting Shaq were obvious. The lone mystery surrounding Shaq was if he possessed the attributes that all the truly great players have — the innate ability to put his team on his back and take it to the promised land. Magic, Larry and Michael (no last names necessary) all had accomplished the task. If Shaq wished to place his name in their lofty company, he'd have to deliver the goods at playoff time, when the pressure is

As Shaq developed a finesse offensive style to complement his power game, the Magic compiled the league's best home record and won their division handily.

enough to make a player's ears pop.

Shaq entered the season carrying enough baggage to fill a jumbo jet. In the time-honored American tradition of building somebody up just to tear them down, the sport of poking holes in Shaq — the man, the myth, the legend — was becoming more and more popular.

The litany of usual complaints had become a chorus. All Shaq could do was dunk. He spends too much time selling himself instead of working on his game. He's all show and no sub-

stance. He can't even hit free throws.

Oh yeah, and he hasn't won anything in the playoffs.

There was no denying that last part. So far, the postseason had proven to be Shaq-proof. The previous season had ended for the Orlando Magic in embarrassing fashion, getting swept, 3-0, at the hands of the Indiana Pacers in the opening round of the playoffs. It was a stunning rebuke for the NBA's Young Guns squad. And Shaq, being the biggest target around at 7-feet, 303

pounds, took the most heat. Forget that he was already a two-time All-Star, had been third in the league's MVP voting the season before and had led Dream Team II to a title at the world championships.

So the '94-95 season became all about making believers. During the summer of 1994, Shaq gave the rest of the league a subtle clue of what was to come. On his right biceps, he got a tattoo of an outstretched hand cradling a globe, with the words: THE WORLD IS MINE. The NBA should have considered itself warned.

With precious little hype, and in a workmanlike fashion, Shaq then went out and dominated every facet of the game during the regular season in his familiar in-your-face, down-your-throat dominance. O'Neal averaged a league-leading 29.3 points a game, as well as 11.4 rebounds (to rank No. 3 in the NBA). Defenders washed up against him in waves, like the sea breaking against the shore. He was double-teamed. He was triple-teamed. Nothing seemed to work.

Only one strategy achieved mixed results: The Hack Shaq Plan. O'Neal was a bricklaying 57 percent free throw shooter for his career, so most nights opponents could force him to pitch a tent at the charity stripe.

But on the whole, Shaq lived up to the tattoo displayed on his other biceps: the Superman logo.

"Hey, Michael [Jordan] is Superman," Shaq says. "I'm just Superboy."

It helped Shaq's cause that the cav-

With playoff veteran Horace Grant at his side, Shaquille helped power the Magic to their first NBA Finals in the team's six-year history.

alry came charging over the hill. Penny Hardaway had a season in the play-for-pay league under his belt. But more importantly, the Magic added Horace Grant to the roster. Not only did the begoggled Grant fill a large hole at power forward, but he gave the young Magic kids somebody to look up to for guidance.

Although the regular season victories piled up, including an astonishing 39-2 record at home, Shaq still would have to wait at least another year before the league's top honor — MVP — would be bestowed upon him. San Antonio's David Robinson received the award instead.

But Shaq was philosophical about it: "They'll have to give it to me someday," he said.

Despite his team's gaudy record, Shaq was well aware of the fact that the regular season is considered just the warm-up act. The playoffs are the main event.

And when the Magic lost at home to the mediocre Boston Celtics in Game 2 of their first-round series, the critics again came out in force, dubbing Shaq and his mates The Not Ready For Prime Time Players.

Then suddenly, the Magic grew up. They became Boyz II Men. They pol-ished off the Celtics with two wins on the famed parquet floor to close out the Boston Garden. Then, in the matchup NBA officials and television executives had dreamed of, the Magic met the Chicago Bulls in Round 2. It was a clash of the titans — Shaq vs. Michael — and a lot of observers believed His Airness, fresh out of retirement, would put the Shaq Attaq in its place.

Wrong.

The Magic came away with a convincing 4-2 series victory that sent Michael to the golf course. It also set up a confrontation that gave Shaq and Orlando a chance to exorcise some demons: the Indiana Pacers. The Magic players didn't get mad. They just got even. Orlando ushered in the Pacers' summer vacation with a thrilling 4-3 series win.

In short order, Shaq had dispatched the Boston Leprechaun, Air Jordan and Reggie Miller. Not bad for a few weeks of work. In just their sixth season in the league, the Magic had reached the NBA Finals. There awaited the biggest challenge of Shaq's young career: Hakeem Olajuwon.

And even before the championship series, Hakeem was offering a few words for all those people who'd spent endless hours trying to find fault with Shaq's game: Get a clue.

Shaquille and the Magic piloted their fans to cloud nine after winning the Eastern Conference title with a Game 7 victory over the Pacers.

"I have a lot of respect for Shaq, just on how he came into the league and established his position right away," Hakeem explained. "People criticize him that he's not developing different moves. But the guy has led the league in scoring. To see a guy that size moving the way he does, you can't compare any player to him."

The frightening bottom line from Shaq's third season is this: He's only going to get better. And the Magic, as a team, also will only get better. This is the dawning not of the age of Aquarius, but rather of the age of the Orlando Magic. Their reign of terror is about to start.

"This is just the beginning for him, and he's already in a class by himself," Hakeem added. "I think he will win many championships and every award there is to win, not only one time, but for many, many years."

The tattoo on Shaq's arm is correct. It is his world. The rest of the NBA is just living in it. •

Mark Emmons is a sports columnist for the Mesa (Ariz.) Tribune.

GLOBAL WARMING

BY BART HUBBUCH

**Shaq's first opportunity
to perform on an international
stage raised the temperature of
his already fevered following**

For 11 days in the summer of 1994, Shaquille O'Neal overshadowed the world — the World Championship of Basketball, that is.

Exploiting the showcase the international tournament provided for his wondrous basketball skills and magnetic personality, Shaq ruled the spotlight on and off the court during his nearly two-week stay in Canada.

Although O'Neal traveled to Toronto as part of Dream Team II, no one doubted which player the record crowds filled SkyDome to see, many for the first time in person.

Everyone wanted a glimpse of Shaq, even if it cost hundreds — or, in some cases, thousands — of dollars to get inside.

Once there, the large contingent of foreign fans responded by giving O'Neal a rousing ovation each time he entered the game and standing ovations for virtually every one of

his countless dunks.

Although such spectacles were nothing new in the United States, the fact that Shaq created such a scene in an otherwise hockey-mad country offered further proof that Shaq's global popularity was firmly on the rise.

"I wasn't really surprised by the attention, but it's nice to know the [international] popularity is there," said O'Neal, who kept his public comments to a minimum during the tournament.

As in the States, Shaq faced mobs of autograph seekers, who congregated at the team's posh hotel in downtown Toronto. He then was mobbed by the huge throng of reporters present after every game and practice.

Fans were just as enthusiastic about anything and everything bearing O'Neal's name or likeness. Replicas of Shaq's Orlando Magic and Team USA jerseys easily were the hottest-selling items during the tournament.

But O'Neal shrugged off the uproar, or at least claimed to be indifferent to it after being named Most Valuable Player and earning first-team all-tournament honors. In doing so, he led the United States to merely its third championship in the 40-year history of the competition.

"Now that we've won the gold medal, I just want to get home, relax and enjoy it," Shaq said after Dream Team II's 137-91 blowout of Russia in the title game. "That's all I'm thinking about."

Even for a 7-1, 300-pounder, O'Neal left quite an impression in Toronto, dominating every center he faced in the 16-team field.

Adequate competition for Shaq was so hard to find that Team USA coach Don Nelson took it easy on the rest of the world. Since the outcomes were never in doubt, O'Neal rarely played more than 20 minutes in any of the United States' eight games.

As a result, Shaq didn't post his usual overwhelming numbers, averaging a mere — at least for O'Neal — 18.0 points, 8.3 rebounds and 2.0 blocked shots per game.

Shaq provided a typical — and typically amazing — performance in the internationally televised title game. He didn't start and played just 16 minutes, but pounded the Russians anyway with 18 points and 10 rebounds.

In fact, O'Neal was so overpowering he had trouble maintaining his concentration at times. That would explain the

Shaq's dominance at the World Championships was so thorough that he averaged barely more than 20 minutes of playing time per game for the tournament.

momentary slipup early in the championship game, when Russian center Vitali Nosov blocked two of Shaq's shots.

But that lapse didn't diminish Shaq's virtual ownership of the tournament, Nelson says.

"Somebody asked me if there were any surprises, and I said, 'Shaq O'Neal is better than I even thought,' " the veteran coach says. "He's certainly one of the greatest players to come along in a long, long time. If he has longevity, he'll be rated right up there with Bill Russell, Wilt Chamberlain, Wes Unseld and some of the great centers."

Perhaps the only surprise of Shaq's trip to Canada was that he dominated despite back stiffness that had developed a month before the tournament and bothered him throughout.

The pain flared early in the tournament, forcing O'Neal to leave some games and do stretching exercises.

"It was kind of sore, but there was never any question that I could still play," Shaq says. "I wanted the gold medal. I could always take a couple of weeks off after the tournament."

Back problems didn't keep O'Neal from having fun, either. His flashiest moment came as the buzzer sounded in Team USA's opening-round romp over Brazil, when Shaq threw the ball against the backboard and then slammed it through the basket.

The crowds loved O'Neal's showmanship — and so did his teammates.

"It's not just the fact that he's a great player," Nelson says. "It's on and off the court. Just being around him, you find out that he's a pretty special person."

Indeed, Shaq kept the rest of Dream Team II entertained with his behind-the-scenes antics, which included an impromptu rap song in the locker room just before the championship game against Russia.

Throughout the tournament, teammates said O'Neal always was ready with a joke, prank or musical interlude.

That in itself was somewhat amazing, considering most players who endure such an unforgiving spotlight usually withdraw, keeping their emotions to themselves. Not Shaq.

"I really feel for him, because it's quite difficult for a man of that stature and that size to have a life," Nelson says. "But he deals with it as well as anyone I've ever seen."

Says New Jersey Nets forward Derrick Coleman, one of O'Neal's Team USA counterparts: "Shaq's a fun guy."

Not to mention a world-class talent.   •

Bart Hubbuch covers the NBA for the Akron *(Ohio)* Beacon Journal.

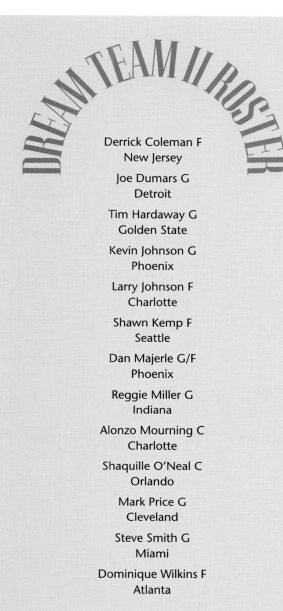

DREAM TEAM II ROSTER

Derrick Coleman F
New Jersey

Joe Dumars G
Detroit

Tim Hardaway G
Golden State

Kevin Johnson G
Phoenix

Larry Johnson F
Charlotte

Shawn Kemp F
Seattle

Dan Majerle G/F
Phoenix

Reggie Miller G
Indiana

Alonzo Mourning C
Charlotte

Shaquille O'Neal C
Orlando

Mark Price G
Cleveland

Steve Smith G
Miami

Dominique Wilkins F
Atlanta

ANDREW BERNSTEIN / NBA PHOTOS

Shaq's golden aura showed in Toronto.

Winning

By Tim Povtak

United as if by magic, Shaquille O'Neal and Anfernee Hardaway since have exhibited a special ability to cast their spell over the entire league

Combination

They are a match made in basketball heaven, a fit any tailor would love, two stars whose talents lock like pieces of an intricate jigsaw puzzle. The luck of the draft lottery brought them together, but a quest to make history will bond them throughout their NBA careers.

Shaquille O'Neal, 23, is the center with an unprecedented combination of size (7-1, 300 pounds) and athletic ability. Anfernee "Penny" Hardaway, 23, is the prototype modern point guard who creates with the flair of an artist. He's the perfect complement to O'Neal — a player with equally impressive, but vastly different, basketball skills.

Together, they are expected to work magic.

The point guard/center combination of stars is not unusual, but the likelihood of it spanning a decade or more is rare. The Hardaway/O'Neal tandem already enjoys comparisons to the fabled Magic Johnson/Kareem Abdul-Jabbar "Showtime" union of the Los Angeles Lakers in the '80s.

Johnson and Abdul-Jabbar played in nine All-Star Games together, and won five NBA titles. O'Neal and Hardaway made their first dual appearance in the starting lineup for the Eastern Conference All-Star team in 1995.

O'Neal and Hardaway form the foundation of the increasingly fearsome Orlando Magic, but they also are expected to bear the banner of the NBA through the turn of the century. Apart, each would have found his own basketball stardom. Together, they are expected to set the course of the NBA, feeding off each other into the next century, complementing their way to a string of world championships.

This horse and carriage combination promises a ride for the long haul.

If O'Neal is the thoroughbred, then Hardaway is the jockey securely handling the reins. One can't win the derby without the other. Although both are stars in their own right, they understand winning NBA titles will require mutual sacrifice and teamwork.

Hardaway directs an abundantly talented Magic team like a conductor directs his symphony, thoroughly pleased when it plays in sync and everyone works together. He starts the game waiting to see what the Magic need each night, then plugs himself in.

O'Neal loves to dunk and to dominate. Hardaway happily provides him with the opportunity. O'Neal may be the team's main attraction, but Hardaway actually can be more entertaining. O'Neal is overpowering, Hardaway dazzling and delightful.

"I know his every move, his every expression now," Hardaway said in the midst of the 1995 playoffs. "I know where he likes the ball and how to get it to him. After playing with him for a couple of years, we don't need to talk. We just know."

Hardaway, at 6-7, 200 pounds, has a style of play that's part Scottie Pippen and part Magic Johnson. He passes, he scores, he rebounds, he defends. And, most importantly, he gets the ball to O'Neal.

What makes the two rare as a point guard/center combination is their ability to run a fast break with either one handling the ball, and with either one on the wing.

More frightening to opponents, both can start or finish an alley-oop dunk.

"I knew what Penny could do before we even got him," O'Neal says.

"And he's been everything we expected. He makes my job easier.

"He's the kind of point guard any center would love to play with," he adds. "He gets you the ball where you need it. We'll win some championships together. How many? I don't know."

O'Neal provides all the inside power any team could want. Last season, he led the league in scoring from the first month to the last. He's strong enough to muscle his way to the basket and agile enough to maneuver into position. The only real weakness to his game is at the free-throw line, but considering his young age, almost everyone believes that will change in the coming years.

"You can't have two better positions [point guard and center] to get great players to build your team around," says Knicks head coach Pat Riley, who coached the Johnson/Abdul-Jabbar combination. "I had it with the Lakers, and it worked out pretty well for us. The Magic have planted a wonderful seed by getting those two together at this stage of their careers."

Although they fit so well, they are opposites in emotion and temperament. O'Neal lights up a room with his smile and mugs for the cameras. Hardaway avoids the bright lights, preferring peace and quiet to the crowd that O'Neal enjoys. Shaq thrives on the glare. Hardaway wears the shades. O'Neal makes rap music and videos. Hardaway would rather sit back, listen and watch.

With Johnson and Abdul-Jabbar, it was just the opposite. The point guard was charismatic, the center reflective and sometimes withdrawn.

"I like to entertain on the court, but most of all I want to win, and I'll do

Although known primarily for wreaking havoc on offense, O'Neal and Hardaway can be just as dominating defensively.

• 41 •
SHAQUILLE O'NEAL

BOB GREENE

The first time they met, Shaquille O'Neal and Anfernee Hardaway were just basketball babes. And it was success at first sight.

The time was 1990, and they were teammates on the South squad at the U.S. Olympic Sports Festival in Minneapolis. Hardaway had just finished high school in Memphis. O'Neal had just completed his freshman year at Louisiana State. Neither knew much about the other. But it didn't take them long to learn.

The South easily won the gold medal. O'Neal set a Sports Festival record for points and rebounds. Hardaway played a key role amassing assists. Even when they hardly knew each other, they worked magic on the basketball court.

They dominated individually and as teammates, although neither thought they'd play together again.

"Shaq made you laugh back then," Hardaway recalls. "He was a comedian, even when he didn't try to be one. I just remember how funny it was watching him dance around the hallway where we stayed. I never knew anyone 7 feet tall and 300 pounds could dance. He was a sight."

Three years later, they were rejoined on the set of *Blue Chips*, the basketball movie starring Nick Nolte and O'Neal. Hardaway played a minor role in the movie, but his appearance played a major part in his

BOB GREENE

future.

Filming took place a month before the 1993 NBA draft. O'Neal was coming off his Rookie of the Year season and being hailed as the league's newest superstar. Hardaway, a junior, already had announced his intention to leave Memphis State.

The Magic had just won the draft lottery and the right to make the first selection. O'Neal had talked about the Magic taking Michigan's highly touted power forward Chris Webber, setting up the NBA's front line of the future. O'Neal couldn't wait for the draft.

But a funny thing happened on the movie set. Hardaway dazzled O'Neal with his passing and ball handling and with his ability to find Shaq anywhere on the court. They

Two encounters before O'Neal and Hardaway linked up in Orlando provided previews to the feature presentation ahead

ComingAttract

whatever the team needs to accomplish that," Hardaway says. "We've had a good start in Orlando, but we really haven't accomplished anything yet. We will before it's over."

Together they are versatile enough to dominate a fast-paced game or adapt to a slow-down affair. Hardaway, despite his youth, is beginning to run the break as well as any point guard in the league. O'Neal is an anchor to the half-court game, almost a throwback to the centers who loved playing close to the basket as opposed to the modern versions who often roam the perimeter.

"The big guy [O'Neal] is such a presence on his own, and Hardaway is mastering things now," Seattle coach George Karl says. "So many times, I look at them and think they look like Magic Johnson and Kareem Abdul-Jabbar playing together again. They are playing at that high of a plateau."

O'Neal and Hardaway first were

Shaq and Penny figure to have much to celebrate during the years ahead.

talked about having won the gold medal at the Sports Festival three years before. They talked about playing together again. They talked about winning an NBA championship.

O'Neal called the Magic front office officials, just to let them know what he thought about Hardaway. Maybe Webber wasn't their best choice after all.

On draft day, the Magic selected Webber with the No. 1 pick, but then immediately traded him to Golden State for Hardaway (the No. 3 selection) and three future first-round picks.

The rest is history, which is what the two hope to make more of before their NBA careers are finished.

— *Tim Povtak*

ions

FERNANDO MEDINA

united on the South team at the 1990 United State Olympic Festival in Minneapolis. They played together again on the production set of *Blue Chips*, the basketball movie featuring Nick Nolte

When it comes to attracting attention, Shaq towers over Hardaway, but Penny prefers the shadows to the limelight.

that was filmed in the summer of 1993. O'Neal, who had just finished his rookie season in the NBA, had a starring role. Hardaway, who'd just left Memphis State, played a minor part. But their time on the set was when O'Neal really saw what Hardaway could do — and it had nothing to do with acting. Upon returning to Orlando, Shaq encouraged the Magic to draft or trade for Hardaway. He knew

a good thing when he saw it.

"Now I've got pennies from heaven," O'Neal says with a smile. "We made the right move. He is the real thing. You could see that from the time he arrived."

The mere presence of a great point guard makes a great center even better, creating space and opportunities by causing problems on the perimeter that defenses can't ignore. The presence of a great center also helps a point guard immensely in an opposite way. It gives him more space to create.

"When you have a great big man, the next thing you look for is the point guard," Magic head coach Brian Hill says. "Then you build your team by filling in the pieces around them. It's like putting together a baseball team: You start up the middle with pitcher, catcher, shortstop, second baseman and center fielder. In basketball, you start at center and point guard. Barring any injuries or unforeseen problems, I could see our two guys playing together as All-Stars for years to come."

The Magic already have been adamant about ensuring the two finish their careers together. O'Neal just finished the third year of a seven-year contract, but the Magic have discussed extending it this summer, providing him with the league's first $100 million pact. Hardaway just finished the first year of a nine-year contract that could be worth up to $70 million.

Creating a winning point guard/center combination is the biggest reason the Magic made the controversial trade on draft day 1993, when they obtained the rights to the lesser-known Hardaway by trading more highly touted power forward Chris Webber, whom they selected with the No. 1 pick, to Golden State.

JERRY WACHTER

STEVE LIPOFSKY

Magic fans hope it's a long way off, but one day they'll likely marvel at the legacy O'Neal and Hardaway have left behind.

Spurring the transaction was the belief that neither O'Neal nor Webber could reach their maximum potential playing together, but that O'Neal and Hardaway could climb to the stars together. That trade now looks like a

stroke of genius.

Although fans initially booed the trade at Orlando Arena when it first was announced — and Hardaway later received a chilly early reception from the home fans — both Penny and Shaq now have captivated the city of Orlando and represent the league's biggest drawing card. The Magic already are the league's most popular team. Now they're trying to become its best team. Last season,

Webber was traded to Washington.

"It's almost unheard of, to get two great players — a center and a point guard — like this at such a young age," Magic assistant coach Richie Adubato says. "They can be so good, it's almost frightening. No question, they are super talents. The only thing you have to realize, though, is that it takes a little time." •

Tim Povtak covers the NBA for The Orlando Sentinel.

At every stop around the NBA, Shaq-mania swirls around the Magic and their larger-than-life centerpiece

ROAD
SHOW

His video claims he's larger than life. That goes double for Shaquille O'Neal when he and the Magic hit the road. Traveling with the NBA's most recognizable rapper is like going on tour with a rock megastar. And the scene swirling around the Magic's road show, with Shaq at the eye of

the storm, has become so crazy the Magic now employs a security consultant as part of the team's traveling party. It's his job to help deal with the swarms of fans who inevitably wait in front of every hotel, in every lobby and outside every arena.

In only a year-plus of traveling with O'Neal, Sgt. Mike Cofield of the Orange County (Fla.) Sheriff's office has witnessed some baffling sights.

"I'm constantly running people off the players' floor at their hotels," Cofield says. "People now will even check into the team hotel, just so they can see them. We got into one place at 2:30 in the morning, and a 5-year-old was waiting with his dad. 5 years old!"

Whether he's posing in front of the Parthenon in Athens or signing autographs on an American streetcorner, Shaq is a magnet for attention.

Of course, these bizarre incidents didn't happen before the Magic hit the jackpot and selected O'Neal with the No. 1 overall pick in the 1992 NBA

BILL FRAKES / SPORTS ILLUSTRATED

• 47 •
SHAQUILLE O'NEAL

draft. Before then, the Magic traveled in relative calm. And they flew commercial. Along with O'Neal, not so coincidentally, came the franchise's first team plane.

"Can you see Shaq having to wait around in an airport?" Magic forward Jeff Turner asks. "I don't think he could even walk from his car to the gate. He'd be mobbed."

It'd be something akin to, say, Michael Jackson, if he decided to take a casual stroll to a commercial jet to whisk him off to his next concert.

"Can you imagine how long it would take Shaq to walk through the terminal if we still flew commercial?" Magic head coach Brian Hill asks. "There's almost no way we'd be able to handle that situation."

Because of Shaq's worldwide appeal and fame, the team tends to avoid staying at hotels with open atriums and glass elevators, because overzealous fans will watch players go up, then follow them to their rooms.

It's been rumored that once, O'Neal heard a knock at his hotel room door and opened it only to find a young woman standing there clad in a raincoat — and nothing else. O'Neal sheepishly declines to comment on the story.

But the intense fan adulation that inspires such crazy anecdotes is the same everywhere the Magic visit.

"I hear the same thing from all the security people at hotels — that they can't believe the crowds this team draws," Cofield says. "And these are hotels that are used to dealing with movie stars and politicians. They just can't get over the reaction this team gets. And it's everywhere we go."

Like most of the NBA's other superstars, O'Neal is registered under an alias at every hotel the Magic stay in. But this doesn't stop fans from disturbing other members of the team's traveling

Shaq reluctantly endures the endless series of bus rides that are the bane of NBA life, because the benefits of travel sometimes produce magical moments.

party, oftentimes posing as family, friends or fraternity brothers and claiming they desperately need to speak with Shaq.

"I tell them, 'If you're really Shaq's friend, you'd know how to get in touch with him,' " says Magic assistant coach Tree Rollins, who doubles as O'Neal's backup at center.

Even the world's most recognized athlete, Michael Jordan, has the option of slipping on a hat and sunglasses and partially hiding his identity if he wants to go out in public. But there's no phone booth where the NBA's version of Superman can change. He's just too big.

"I could make a disguise — but I'm 7-1," O'Neal laughs.

Fully aware of the consequences, O'Neal occasionally will hit a nearby shopping mall with good friend and teammate Dennis Scott, the Magic's starting small forward. Both players are renowned practical jokers and enjoy shopping for high-tech gadgets they can use to trick their teammates.

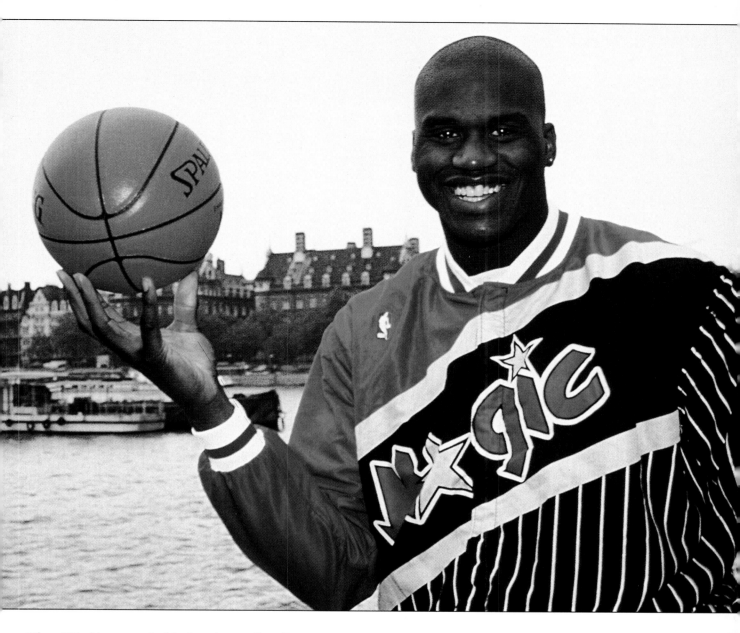

When O'Neal is approached by fans, he usually will sign autographs graciously, as long as he's not interrupted while doing something else.

"What Shaq can do is limited," Scott says. "But even as big a star as he is, he can still go out, as long as there's communication. He just tells people he's trying to shop like a regular person, and most people appreciate that."

Once in a while, O'Neal and Scott bravely will check out nightspots around the NBA circuit. This, of course, takes careful planning — a limousine and some burly attendants, for starters. Scott says Shaq tends to steer toward the cautious side. After all, he's a walking, not to mention unmistakable, target.

"Definitely, with Shaq, you can't put him in a situation where there's an overload of people," Scott says. "And most cities, on Friday and Saturday nights, are just packed. That makes it difficult."

But, hey, that's the price of fame. So, instead of dealing with the madness that inevitably awaits him everytime he steps out in public, this fun-loving 23-year-old with loads of money to spend and plenty of travel opportunities frequently winds up in his hotel room, about the only place he can get a little privacy.

"I stay in and watch SpectraVision," says Shaq, who claims he once watched Jurassic Park three times in one day.

"It's tough," Scott says. "I can't imagine being him. You can never have a normal life. But, you know, Shaq handles it really well."

Good thing, because for Shaq, the road show must go on. •
Susan Slusser covers the Magic for The Orlando Sentinel.

POWERFUL IMAGES

Just as his forceful feats on the

basketball court elicit strong

reactions from fans and opponents,

Shaq inspires similar emotions from

those who try to capture his

essence with oils and inks. Artistic

representations of Shaq typically

are as robust as his game.

ED GRAGG

SHAQUILLE O'NEAL

ALAN STUDT

AMY CHENIER

ALAN STUDT

SHAQUILLE O'NEAL

JOHN PATTERSON

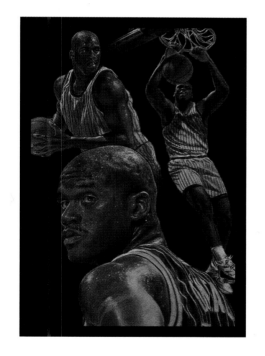

JAMES LeMASURIER

STEVEN STEGALL

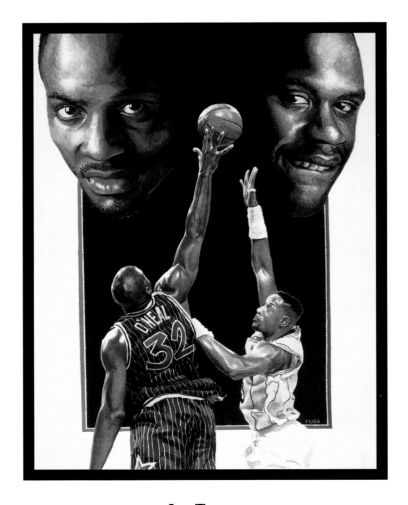

JAY TYSVER

BILL WADDLE

ED GRAGG

SHAQUILLE O'NEAL

DAN SMITH

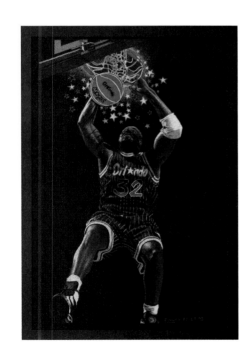

CHUCK FEIST

FEEDING Frenzy

Shaq's appetite for destruction has many centers around the league feeling hunger pangs

By Mike Kahn

O nly a moment or two on the basketball court with Shaquille O'Neal is required to learn that neither you eyes, nor videos, tell lies.

He is indeed 7-1 and all of 303 pounds, sporting the agility to bounce around the low post or a rap concert.

How far he can carry the Orlando Magic remains to be seen. O'Neal is eyeing a championship, but then, he's always set lofty

EYE TO EYE
with Shaq
By Hakeem Olajuwon

(as told to Robert Falkoff)

Whenever I take the court against Shaquille, the first thing I notice is his size. He's a legitimate 300-pound man. A giant. I always have to be aware of his tremendous power. Plus, he's very quick and agile.

As a result, I have to do a lot of extra work against him. Not only must I establish position, but I've got to realize that I can't let down for one second or he'll take advantage.

On defense, the thing everybody has to stop first is the dunk. That's Shaquille's basic shot right now — and you can't get any more basic than that. If you don't keep a body on him, he'll dunk so hard he'll break the backboard.

The best all-around big man in the game today marvels at the ability Shaq brings to the table.

With Shaquille, you also must be aware of his jump hook. It's part of his arsenal now, but he still has to work on it more and more until the shot comes naturally.

I don't think he needs to use my basic shot, the drop-step jumper, that much — mainly because of his size and power. Although I need the drop-step jumper to get my shot off, Shaquille can just take one step and jump over people. He can shoot the drop-step, but it's really just a matter of how much he wants to use it. He doesn't really need the "Dreamshake."

When I'm on offense and he's on defense, the thing that sticks out is his instinct for blocking shots. Shaquille has tremendous reflexes. If you beat him, he can recover quickly. You can take him out of the play with a good move, and he can get back into it with those great reflexes. It's natural.

I've never seen a 300-pound guy that quick. I've gone against other 300-pound guys, such as Mark Eaton, who have the strength but not the agility. In that case, you have to go around him. With Shaquille, you can't just make up your mind you're going around him or over him. You have to pick your spots and be patient, looking for just the right opening.

Other parts of his game also are impressive. He's very aggressive as a rebounder, using his body to keep people off the boards and out of the paint. And he makes good decisions as a passer and has a feel for where to go with the ball.

The one aspect that would help round out Shaquille's game is improved free-throw shooting, because he's going to get fouled a lot. When I came into the league 11 years ago, I was in the same position. I had to become a better foul shooter and I've worked very hard at it. Shaquille has a nice touch; he just needs to soften it up a little.

The more free throws he shoots, the more Shaquille will work to raise the percentage. Once he does that, the sky is the limit for what he can accomplish.

To sum it all up, I know I'm going against the best competition when I'm going against Shaquille O'Neal. It's always a war, from start to finish. And no doubt Shaquille deserves the attention he gets. He is the future of this league. •

Robert Falkoff covers the Rockets for the Houston Post.

goals. When he needed to improve his offensive skills between years one and two, Shaq rose to the challenge.

"Already, I see a different player," Kevin Loughery said at the time. "He's got more of a game inside than last year. He was more predictable [last season]. So far this year, he's showing everybody a little bit more."

Most of the people experiencing this new-and-improved Shaq are NBA centers, those unlucky men who each night look the big guy right in the eye . . . and blink.

Until recently, big men hadn't been the NBA's center of attention. Throughout the 1980s and into the 1990s, the league's headliners were shooting guards such as Michael Jordan and Clyde Drexler, point guards such as Magic Johnson and Isiah Thomas, and power forwards such as Karl Malone and Charles Barkley. Unless your name was Patrick, David or Hakeem, earning a paycheck playing center meant two things — clogging the paint on defense and getting out of the way on offense.

But Shaq has turned the focus back to the men in the middle. He's made playing center a glamour job again.

Because of Shaq's immense celebrity status outside of the game and responsibilities for endorsements and assorted league and team appearances, cynics waited to see if O'Neal worked on

LAYNE MURDOCH

Trying to prevent O'Neal from dunking is like stepping in front of a runaway freight train.

his game at all during his first professional off-season. Most people didn't even notice he spent one week at Pete Newell's Big Man's Camp.

"I sure knew he was there," Seattle forward Shawn Kemp says. "Shaq worked as hard as anybody there. We played against each other a lot. He's so strong and he's got a lot better skills at the post than a lot of people give

him credit for."

Some of O'Neal's opponents already have noticed the improvement in his game. It's startling to see this 23-year-old monster gaining finesse on top of all that strength.

"He surprised me," Detroit Pistons head coach Don Chaney says. "He made a move to the basket off the dribble and made a running

EYE TO EYE with Shaq

By Brad Daugherty

(as told to Joe Menzer)

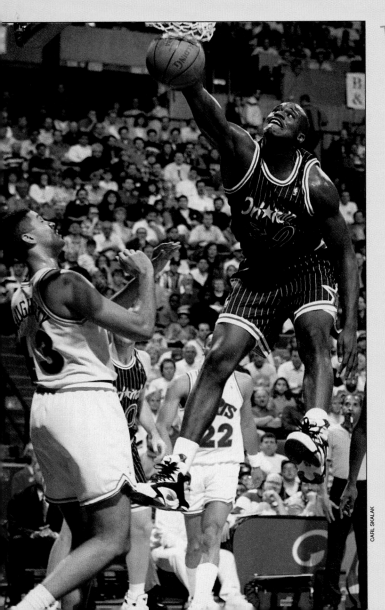

Known for his superb passing, Daugherty is quick to dish out kudos to No. 32.

Less than a third of the way into his career, Shaquille O'Neal already ranks among the top two or three centers in the NBA — at least as far as I'm concerned. The reasons are simple: He's so much stronger and younger than everybody else, and he's got a great attitude.

Sure, Shaquille doesn't own the experience that some of us other big guys have. But he'll get that in time. Besides, Shaquille possesses some qualities that none of us ever will be able to acquire.

His ability? Nobody can match it, except maybe Patrick Ewing and Hakeem Olajuwon. And even those guys can't combine the physical package of 7 feet and 300-plus pounds with the explosiveness that makes Shaquille so tough.

Hakeem is pretty heavy. Patrick is big and solid, but not as big as Shaquille. And Patrick doesn't quite have the same explosiveness that Shaquille has. Plus, we're all older, so Shaquille has youth on his side. He has that extra spring in his step.

I suppose the main thing that overwhelms you is Shaquille's size. He's so big, yet there isn't an ounce of fat on this guy. Although he's already a super player, I think if Shaquille continues to polish his post moves and develops what I call "touch shots," he'll really have the whole package.

To defend Shaquille, big people on opposing teams will likely just collapse around him to prevent him from dunking the ball. Thus, to offset those kinds of defenses, Shaquille will have to develop touch shots around the goal to be more effective.

Should Shaquille do that, he'll probably become the greatest big man ever to play the game.

But don't think Shaquille just throws the ball up there now and goes after it. All of his moves already are legitimate — especially for a young guy who in college never consistently played against a lot of other big, bruising guys.

If he can work with someone on developing more moves and improving his footwork, while adding those touch shots, he'll be unstoppable. He's almost unstoppable now.

Like many young big guys on defense, Shaquille tries to block a lot of shots. He does a lot of things you would expect. He tries to watch the play and react according to what he sees happening on the floor.

But he's a big guy back there who takes up a lot of room — so he's got a great presence in the lane. His size alone makes him a factor. He's going to change some shots, even if he doesn't actually block them. That type of presence can change the course of a game.

When I look at Shaquille, it's pretty amazing how big and how quick he is. Three hundred-and-some pounds — that's a lot of pounds to be as quick and move as athletically as he does. Really, that's the most amazing thing about him. That, plus he's only 23 years old. His best years are ahead of him.

If Shaq stays healthy, he could play a long, long time — and do some things in this league that no other big man has done. •

Joe Menzer covers the Cavaliers for the News Herald.

hook another time. Everything I saw [his rookie year] was basically power moves."

Of course, that's what concerns most defenders from the outset. Shaq's incredible strength is the first thing they attempt to neutralize. Veteran Cavs center Michael Cage has his own set of rules when confronted with this colossus. O'Neal's first night of scoring below double-figures can be attributed largely to Cage.

"The key is not to get too technical, and just try to keep him off balance," Cage says. "He's so big and so talented, there's very little you can do if he gets in position at the basket. He'll just overpower you.

"So, you can fight him for post position and try to frustrate him by not letting him plant his foot. You can't let him plant and move in a rhythm. If he does, you're dead. I just keep trying to make him change his steps. At the same time, I don't want him to know where I am, so I try to confuse him.

"But this is going to work only so long. He's just testing the waters now because he's so young. He's going to get better every year, and that's absolutely scary for the rest of the league."

The league already knows O'Neal was ROY at the age of 20, and he's just learning what it's like to play against centers with more experience and bountiful skills.

"The key is not to get too technical, and just try to keep him off balance. He's so big and so talented, there's very little you can do if he gets in position at the basket. He'll just overpower you."

— Cleveland's Michael Cage

ew rookies ever have come into the NBA and equaled his impact of 23.4 points, 13.9 rebounds and 3.5 blocks per game. His major weakness was converting just 59 percent of his foul shots. But even that flaw came with a silver lining. It simply gave basketball historians another reason to compare Shaq to Wilt Chamberlain, the Hall of Fame center who never mastered the free throw.

Coaches already rank O'Neal favorably with Hakeem Olajuwon, David Robinson, Patrick Ewing, Robert Parish and Brad Daugherty as an elite center.

"I would rate him up there," says Houston Rockets head coach Rudy Tomjanovich, who as a young player competed against Chamberlain his final three seasons. "I watched [Shaq] on tapes, and he's really got a lot of tools. He really plays inside

more so than the other centers in the league. He really plays the inside game when he gets the ball deep in the paint.

"The other centers have more of an outside shot, and they'll go to it more. I guess that's an area of less resistance. Ewing has a turn-around that fades a little bit, Parish has it, and Hakeem has it. But right now, Shaq's the guy who's taking it to the basket. He's right up there in the upper echelon of centers of this league already."

Olajuwon would know. He and O'Neal share agent Leonard Armato, so Hakeem played ball with the big guy in the summer of 1992, even before Shaq introduced himself to the rest of the NBA. Needless to say, "The Dream" had an inkling of O'Neal's impact.

"He's strong, he's quick, and he's only going to improve," Olajuwon says. "I've even put a fake on him and

EYE TO EYE
with Shaq

By Robert Parish

(as told to Peter May)

Shaquille O'Neal is going to be one of the great centers in this league. The sky is the limit for him. He's already good, especially for a guy who doesn't have, basketball-speaking, "the basics." He doesn't have a jump shot or a hook shot. He's all power. And yet he still averaged 23.4 points a game his first season. That says something about his athletic ability.

Obviously, to become a great center, he needs a jump shot. That's very important. A hook shot. Or a jump hook. He needs something, because what's going to happen when he can no longer overpower everybody? Then what?

The Chief thought he had seen everything during his 19 seasons on the blocks, but O'Neal's overpowering talents caught even the NBA's elder statesman off guard.

For the time being, he's getting away with brute force. He moves you out of the way. He's kind of like Utah's Mark Eaton — only with athletic skills. Seriously, you just can't do anything about it. At least, I can't. He outweighs me by 70 pounds or more.

When I'm playing Shaquille, I try to push him out as far as I can on the floor. Thus, when he goes in for a shot, he's taking a longer shot. I seem to have success with that. But if he gets the ball around the basket, there's really nothing you can do except hope that he misses. And he usually doesn't miss a dunk.

I remember the first time I played against Shaquille. The thing that went through my mind was how hard his body was. It reminded me of Artis Gilmore. Just completely solid. No soft spots at all. I'd be trying to box him out and I'd bump up against him and he was so solid. He is all man. Definitely.

When Shaquille plays

defense, he's like most shot blockers — they're at their best when they stand still. They wait on you to come in. To counter that, I try to keep him busy and move him around.

Obviously, no one has spent any serious time with him. He's been so overpowering, there has been no need to develop anything. But he really does need a big man to work with exclusively in the off-season. Someone to work with him on the fundamentals of the game, especially on offense. He doesn't have any problems defensively.

Unfortunately, the motivation for practicing and improving is harder to find when you average as many points as Shaquille did in his rookie season. It's easy to say, "Why do I need a jump shot? Why do I need a hook shot?" Think about that. Look what he did his rookie year. I know I'd be asking myself those same questions if I had put up the numbers he did.

But the thing is, when you limit yourself like that, eventually the game catches up with you. Because as you get older, that's when those skills really come into play. After saying all that, however, I still rate Shaquille right up there with the best centers of the last decade. Look at what he's done — and he doesn't even have a jump shot or a hook shot. Think if he just got one of those weapons how tough he would be. It's scary. He averages 25 points a game and can't shoot a lick. Think about that. •

Peter May covers the Celtics for the Boston Globe.

he's so quick, he recovered."

That's the overwhelming part about O'Neal for most players. Other players may be of similar size and bulk, possibly even close in strength. But his quickness is the defining difference.

"He has all of the tools," says Parish, the oldest player in the NBA. "I definitely like his defensive prowess. He's strong, has good timing, and all the shots he doesn't block he alters because of his presence."

Or, as veteran center Anthony Avent put it, "The only way to defend that size lengthwise and widthwise is to be that size."

Talented 7-foot defenders such as Dikembe Mutombo still have an idea of how to at least slow Shaq down.

"He's really good on the inside, but he can be too one-dimensional," Mutombo says. "He needs to develop a more rounded game. When he gets the outside shot, he will create more offensive opportunities for himself."

More? Defenders in general no doubt will provide him with engraved invitations to the perimeter. Offer him gifts to hang with the smaller folks on the floor.

Shaq's most overwhelming quality is his versatility. He can put the ball on the floor, even take it from rim to rim on some occasions. Most

When Shaq puts the heat on by taking matters into his own hands, defenses usually melt.

people believe no one can prevent him from dominating the league except himself.

O'Neal may never have the grace of Kareem Abdul-Jabbar, nor the passing skills of Bill Walton. But he is gifted with the strength, size and presence of Chamberlain on offense and the timing of Bill Russell on defense. As anybody already can tell, that should be enough.

Cleveland Cavaliers general manager Wayne Embry played against Chamberlain and Russell, and was general manager of the Milwaukee Bucks when Abdul-Jabbar played there. He sees O'Neal occupying that same class.

"Shaq definitely is the strongest player in the game

today, like Wilt was in his day. So that makes him almost impossible to stop at the rim," Embry says. "But he also has some of the lateral quickness Russell had to cut off the lane and the base line. Those are gifts. You don't stop people with such gifts. All you can do is hope to confuse them or wear them out."

Good luck.

Shaq isn't easily confused, nor will he likely wear down anytime soon. But you'll have to excuse opposing centers for grasping at straws. When trying to defend against a Shaq attack, that's about all that's left. •

Mike Kahn covers the NBA for the Tacoma Morning News.

SHAQUILLE O'NEAL

WHAT'S next

By Tim Povtak

FERNANDO MEDINA / F.M. ASSOC.

**Shaq's future contains no limits
if the big guy continues what he started**

Think Shaquille O'Neal is popular now? Try looking ahead five years.

On the basketball court, Shaq takes charge as the NBA's dominant force. The skills he continues to develop, combined with his already awesome raw talent, prove unstoppable. And his team, the Orlando Magic, emerges as one of the league's elite, a perennial championship contender.

Off the court, O'Neal looms just as large. No longer just a basketball star, he becomes an international celebrity, perhaps the world's most recognizable sports figure. His rap videos serve as staples of the Hip-Hop generation. Former cameo appearances in movies progress into fullfledged leading roles. Book signings and autograph sessions draw massive crowds. No longer can he walk the streets without worries of crowd control.

Is this what the future holds for O'Neal? Only time will tell. Certainly the big guy is off to a big start.

After just three years in the league, O'Neal already is the game's biggest attraction, one of a handful of players drawing raves in every arena.

Already, his name alone brings smiles to the faces of basketball fans, hobbyists off all ages, card company executives and marketing strategists. The only frowns come from opponents futilely searching for ways to stop him.

"There's no reason why he can't be prolific both on and off the court," says Leonard Armato, O'Neal's agent, attorney

and business adviser. "The possibilities with him are unlimited."

And yet, Shaq just 23 years old. He's only scratched the surface.

"Five years from now, the furor that surrounded the retirement of Michael Jordan will seem secondary compared to the impact Shaq will be having on the league," Orlando general manager Pat Williams predicts. "There won't be anyone else in sports to compare him to."

Shaq's projected impact five years from now may seem like an exaggeration. After all, how much more popular can he become?

Success will play a large part in determining what level of celebrity he reaches. As well as Shaq played during his rookie season, the Magic still failed to make the playoffs. Not only does O'Neal need to lead his team into the postseason, but ultimately he needs to help the Magic win championships — much like Jordan legitimized himself by carrying the Bulls to three consecutive titles.

Timing also is important. An unprecedented combination of size and quickness, with a unique blend of style and substance, O'Neal turned pro just when the NBA stands ready to flex its muscle in the worldwide marketplace.

Larry Bird and Magic Johnson, largely responsible for the popularity the league now enjoys, carried the NBA through the '80s. What they started, Jordan raised to another level while gaining recognition as the greatest player of all time. Yet none of those three, or anyone else before, received the global exposure O'Neal will enjoy throughout his career.

The NBA is moving into Canada with a franchise in Toronto for the 1995-96 season. A second franchise in Vancouver likely isn't far behind. A team in Mexico City, a city of 20 million people, should be next. The NBA plans to open television markets into the Far East, across Europe and well into South America, playing exhibition games almost everywhere to ignite the burgeoning interest.

By the turn of the century, the NBA may have expanded to as many as 36 teams, says commissioner David Stern. The current number is 29.

By then, Shaq will have entered the prime of his career. He'll be ready to explore as many possibilities as time permits.

"People will pay to see him," Philadelphia head coach John Lucas explains. "He has an aura about him that only the greatest have. No one wants to say they were sitting in some

Developing go-to shots such as the fadeaway will lead Shaq to the Hall of Fame. Developing his teammates will lead him to the winner's circle.

PAUL CHAPMAN / F.M. ASSOC.

TIM O'DELL

bar watching a game on TV when he pulled down a backboard. They want to be able to say they had a ticket to the game and were in the arena to see it."

As a player, O'Neal is limited only by his work ethic and by the talent surrounding him. At this point, both variables look promising.

"I'm a little too young to say it now, but I'll be The Man in this league someday. I want to be the best player in the game," O'Neal says. "Five years from now, who knows? I could have one or I could have three NBA titles next to my name. You just never know. I could have retired by then."

O'Neal often half-jokes that his first NBA contract — seven years, $40 million — could be his last. Few take him seriously. The Magic have upgraded the talent around him. And in 1993, Orlando won the draft lottery and traded the rights of top pick Chris Webber to Golden State for the rights to guard Anfernee Hardaway. Many believe the O'Neal-Hardaway twosome is the building block for a championship team.

With other good, young players such as defensive specialist Nick Anderson and sharpshooter Dennis Scott, along with playoff-tested Horace Grant, an important free-agent signee from the Chicago Bulls, the Magic own a bright future.

Only O'Neal's shines brighter.

"Five years from now, he'll be averaging 30 points and 15 to 16 rebounds per game," says Jeff Ruland, a former NBA banger in the paint.

"He'll be a much better passer, able to kill teams who try and double- and triple-team him. He'll be smarter. He's so strong now, but he'll be even bigger and stronger in a few years. It's almost scary."

O'Neal finished his rookie season among the league leaders in scoring (23.4, eighth), rebounding (13.9, second), blocked shots (3.53, second) and field-goal percentage (.562, fourth). But many still considered his game raw.

Certainly, room for improvement exists. His free-throw shooting was a poor 59.2 percent. He fell into constant foul trouble, fouling out eight times. He committed too many turnovers (3.8 average per game), and his offensive game remained limited to in-close power moves to the basket.

He has not yet maximized his skills — and yet, Shaq already has upgraded his game. He was edged out of his first scoring crown by David Robinson on the final day of the 1993-94 season, and won his first scoring title last season.

If O'Neal learns the art of the free throw, NBA defenses will have to go back to the drawing board.

2002: A SHAQ ODYSSEY

Shaquille Rashaun O'Neal

Age: 30   Height: 7-1   Weight: 303   College: LSU

10 All-Star Game Appearances
2 NBA Championships: (1995-96 and 1996-97)
4 NBA MVPs: (1994-1997)
3 All-Star Game MVPs: (1994-95, 1995-96, 1997-98)

Season	G	REB	PTS	AVG	BLKS
1992-1993	81	1,122	1,893	23.4	286
1993-1994	81	1,072	2,377	29.3	231
1994-1995	79	901	2,315	29.3	192
1995-1996	82	1,221	2,753	33.6	299
1996-1997	80	1,106	2,948	36.9	289
1997-1998	78	1,011	2,366	30.3	290
1998-1999	79	1,117	2,551	32.3	286
2000-2001	82	1,224	2,580	31.5	270
2001-2002	80	1,119	2,948	30.3	272
Totals	**803**	**11,497**	**25,135**	**30.3**	**2,710**

After a mere 3 seasons, Shaquille O'Neal has made an impact on the NBA in more ways than anyone could have predicted. Just think of what people will be saying about the big guy after 10 seasons. We thought about it and came up with this special "Fast Forward" card back for the Magic's main man. Although, in our estimation, O'Neal will trail Wilt Chamberlain's blistering scoring pace — Wilt scored 27,098 points after his first 10 seasons — Shaq's numbers definitely should warrant Hall of Fame attention.

No one doubts his future.

"If he stays relatively healthy, I don't see how he can miss becoming the best player in the league," veteran coach Kevin Loughery predicts. "He just has so much going for him. All that size, strength and quickness. Nobody will stop him a few years from now."

Michael Jordan now has company as the game's unofficial spokesman. Charles Barkley would seem the likely successor, if not for his penchant for controversy. Larry Johnson owns plenty of charisma and appeal. But Shaq's man-child quality seems the more natural fit.

O'Neal does not shy away from fame. When the spotlight heats up, Shaq turns on the charm, a characteristic the NBA's marketing arm loves.

If Shaq is successful on the court, his off-court popularity will be easy. The Magic were selected to play an exhibition game in London — the first NBA contest ever in Great Britain — because of O'Neal. When he arrived, his presence drew phenomenal attention.

Newspapers around the country carried full-page pictures of O'Neal. More than 200 journalists appeared at the Magic's first practice, all wanting Shaq interviews. Even more amazing, 2,000 fans waited at a downtown London night spot just to watch O'Neal walk inside for an invitation-only party.

The same fervor rumbled this summer during a promotional tour in Japan, when O'Neal's presence in a shopping mall nearly caused a riot.

"Five years from now, he'll be the one everybody says replaced Michael Jordan in the megastar category," says Stu Inman, a longtime NBA executive. "He'll be the one guy everyone in the NBA just loves, regardless of which team you work for or root for. He's just got a presence about him that will bring him so much."

Five years from now, O'Neal may own a business empire second-to-none in the sports world. He would love to dabble in the entertainment world outside of sports, to produce records and make movies. He wants to become a big-shot businessman.

And he wants to win NBA championships, which would make his other pursuits easier to achieve.

"I don't know if there's anything he won't be able to do," Armato says. "Basketball is his first priority, but there are other things in his life that he still wants to accomplish. And he will."

So far, he's off to a flying start.   •

Tim Povtak covers the Magic for The Orlando Sentinel.

Com

plete
Package

A do-everything center in his time, Hall of Famer Bill Walton thinks Shaq has it all

"Shaquille O'Neal is a player who has come an incredible distance, this season more than ever. The level of superstardom Shaq eventually will attain is finally starting to show.

"I've been working with him and seeing him and watching him play since his sophomore year at LSU, when I went down there to work with him. He's now learning to have a mental impact on the game. He's always been a huge physical star. In fact, he looks the same today that he did six years ago. And not just his running up and down the court, which a lot of players do. Sometimes, they just don't have any sense of control or flow of the game. But right now, he's right there.

"He's got a great franchise around him and great people developing around him. Orlando is

By Bill Walton

building what will be one of the great teams in NBA history.

"Part of his situation is that he got started late playing the game. One of the things that

Bill Walton and Shaquille O'Neal hardly are mirror images of each other with regard to their respective playing styles . . .

MITCHELL B. REIBEL / SPORTS PHOTO MASTERS

helped me and helped so many of the big guys of the era I played in was that guys weren't just recruited because they were big. I grew up playing basketball. I started playing as a guard, and after I grew tall I moved into the post position.

"Now, many players are pulled into the game. They're really big, and their coaches tell them just to go out there and be big and wait for the ball to come to them. And that's supposed to teach them how to play. But where you learn how to play is down at the gym, places like that. A guy such as Shaq can't get that kind of experience today. He'd spend his whole time signing autographs.

"What's really great about Shaq is what a nice person he is and what a hard-working guy he is. A guy such as Shaq could be a big jerk. But he's very humble, caring and a real team player. Just a wonderful person. You can't say enough about him. He works so hard in practice all the time, and he's so inquisitive as to how he can get better. It's a great situation for the NBA, because you've got guys such as him who are so willing to be the great stars of the future.

"His game still is developing. It's a very raw game. It's a different game today than it will be two or three years from now — totally different. When I first went to work with Shaq at LSU — Dale Brown had called me up and asked me to come down — he was teaming with Chris Jackson and Stanley Roberts. Jackson shot every time he touched the ball, and Roberts was taking up the low post on the strong side. Shaq had to play on the weak side and just get rebounds.

"Now, he's the NBA's leading scorer. He's the focal point of that team. He had a career-best season passing the ball. He's sixth in the league in blocks, the team leads the league in road attendance . . . . He has become, well, you can't say he's the No. 1 player because you've still got Jordan out there, but he is the interesting player among all the new guys and with the most potential, the heaviest burden in all of sports.

"Shaq, in a way, is like Wilt and Kareem. The fans always want more. Orlando won 57 games, a franchise record. Shaq had his best season, he led the league in scoring and dominated. And then people bad-mouthed him about his free throws. If we all had such problems in our lives.

"Wilt missed more free throws than anybody. Wilt missed more free throws than most everybody else made. The free throws are a mental thing. Most big guys start out as horrible free-throw shooters. When you're younger, you dominate and win and free throws may not be a factor. But now you get to the NBA, and everybody's very, very good and you hear about it. He will become a much better free-throw shooter. Will he ever shoot 80 percent? I don't know. But even if he did, they'd still foul him every time because two free throws is a lot different than giving up a dunk, which gets the crowd going and tears the game apart.

"In most cases, fans don't always go out to see the big people play. But with Shaq, he has great charisma. Shaq is the combination of Wilt and Magic — the power and the strength, but such a nice guy. And people realize that. You can see it. You don't have the angry young man. He loves to play. And unlike most of the big guys, he is comfortable and relishes the spotlight.

"The potential has been so great for him for so many years that people have been talking to him about his celebrity, explaining that this is going to happen to him, whether he likes it or not. This is the way his life is and how it's going to be. When someone is as famous as he is, you can lose control of your life, but he's done as good a job as can possibly be done. He's doing great.

"With Shaq, you're starting with a great base. Orlando's management is so good. You know they're going to continue to surround him with better players. He's already got some of the best around him. And the fact that they will win so much will help. This is not just a guy averaging 30 or 40 points on a team at the bottom. They're going to be right there. You see it now. It's the superstars. It's a matter of having the great player. That's what you need to win. And Orlando has two in Shaq and Penny Hardaway.

"With Shaq, you're not just going to have one of the great players of all time, but he'll help make Orlando one of the great teams. It's not

there yet, but it will be.

It's all in place. From here on out, it's all mental. Everything will be mental for Shaq. It's not like he's going to have to bulk up or develop.

. . . but Walton, a mentor to Shaq since O'Neal's days at LSU, believes Shaq will become an even greater player than he is now.

ROB TRINGALI JR. / SPORTSCHROME EAST / WEST

He's already there. Now he has to learn how to dominate the league mentally. He's special. •

Hall of Famer Bill Walton dominated the college ranks at UCLA before winning NBA championships in Portland and Boston. He currently covers the NBA for NBC.

Nick Canepa is a sportswriter for the San Diego Union Tribune.

a MAN Among boys

In both high school and college, Shaq clearly stood above the crowd as the country's most awesome talent

BRIAN SPURLOCK

The first time Rusty Segler saw Shaquille O'Neal was on a scouting trip to an undersized gymnasium at Lackland Air Force Base in San Antonio, Texas. Segler, whose Liberty Hill High School team was scheduled to meet O'Neal's San Antonio Cole squad that weekend in a 1988 regional playoff game, didn't know whether to feel awed or awful.

"On that court, it looked like it took him about four strides to get from one end to the other," recalls Segler, now coaching at Concordia Lutheran College in Austin, Texas. "And the ball looked like the smaller women's basketball in his hands. I turned to a friend and said, 'There's no way, man.' I'd never seen anything like him before."

As it turned out, there was a way.

O'Neal, the proverbial bull in a china shop, picked up four fouls in the first five minutes. By the time Shaq returned late in the third quarter, Liberty had built a 15-point lead that Cole couldn't overcome. The 79-74 decision in the Class 2A regional championship was the only loss in O'Neal's two-season, 69-game reign of terror in the Texas high school ranks.

But even the one high school coach who overcame the O'Neal mystique

By Randy Riggs

never has forgotten that first glimpse.

"After I got over the initial shock of seeing him for the first time, one thing became quickly obvious to me," Segler says. "That Cole team was good, but they won a lot of games before they ever tipped off. One look at Shaq was just about all it took."

Cole High's Dave Madura never had coached anyone like O'Neal. In

When LSU failed to win a national championship with its basketball prodigy in the middle, Tigers head coach Dale Brown took the brunt of the criticism.

fact, the 24-year coaching veteran retired after Shaq led the Cougars to an undefeated season (36-0) and a state championship as a senior.

First at Cole and then at LSU, Shaq was a man among boys. But his legacy of intimidating dominance definitely was a double-edged sword.

"Having the opportunity to coach Shaquille was something wonderful that I'll never forget," LSU head coach Dale Brown says. "But there was a downside, too. When we didn't meet the expectations as a team that others imposed on us simply because of Shaquille's presence, it was either, 'Well, Shaquille's not

as good as he's cracked up to be,' or 'Brown must not be much of a coach if he can't win with that guy.' So there was an enormous amount of publicity and pressure, but it was a wonderful experience."

The story of how Brown first stumbled across O'Neal has grown to nearly legendary proportions. On a visit to Germany to conduct a clinic at a U.S. Army base, Brown was approached by a tall youngster wanting to know a proper weight program to build up his leg strength. Although Shaquille already stood at 6-8, he couldn't dunk because he was bothered by Osgood-Schlatter's disease, which weakens the knees.

Brown asked the youngster how long he'd been in the military. Shaquille sheepishly replied that he was just 13 years old.

Brown's next question?

"Can I meet your father?"

Sgt. Philip Harrison, a career military man, was transferred from Germany to Fort Sam Houston in San Antonio in the spring of 1987, O'Neal's sophomore year in high school. At Cole, which has an enrollment primarily of children of military personnel, it didn't take long for word to reach Madura that the new kid in school was definitely worth checking out.

"A football coach came running in and said, 'Geez, we've got a 6-10 kid in school,' " Madura recalls. "I walked down to the cafeteria to take a look and I knew right away this kid was going to be a basketball player."

O'Neal's reputation grew almost as fast as he did.

Not long into his junior year, he already was being compared to the greatest players ever to come out of Texas — the Larry Johnsons and the LaBrad-

BRIAN TIRPAK

"Your Ball, YOUR COURT, Your Game!"

This one sentence, drilled into Shaq by his dad, has been the big guy's motto ever since he stepped onto the basketball court

A kid up to no good. A parent too busy to care.

For a disturbingly large number of kids in the United States, this scenario plays itself out every day.

For Shaquille O'Neal, a kid constantly looking for trouble — and finding it — in his preteen years, one rock-solid factor steered him in the right direction. Thanks to his father, Philip Harrison, Shaquille now is making statistics instead of being one.

Harrison is a nononsense disciplinarian who just recently retired from the military after 20 years of service. Because of the nature of his job, Sgt. Harrison's family constantly was on the move.

Shaq was born in Newark, N.J., moved to Bayonne, N.J., in the first grade, and was in Eatontown, N.J., by the third grade. Halfway through Shaquille's fifth-grade year, the family moved to Fort Stewart, Ga. Then, just as Shaq got comfortable in the sixth grade, the family moved to Germany. The constant uprooting was a strain on the youngster. But his father wouldn't tolerate insubordination.

"He was tough on me as a kid, and I needed it," Shaquille says. "I was pretty much a juvenile delinquent when we lived in New Jersey and Germany. I stole things, broke things and got into fights all the time. I hated living in Germany so much that I tried everything I could to force him to send me back to the States. But he never let me go back."

Like many fathers, Harrison was his son's first coach. He drilled Shaquille on the old Boston Celtics/Red Auerbach system.

"He'd have me pop out at the top of the key and look inside for an open man," O'Neal says in his book, *Shaq Attaq!* "He didn't want me standing under the basket and taking easy shots just because I was taller than everyone else."

Of course, his coaches since then haven't minded taking advantage of Shaq's considerable size. But Harrison wanted his son to learn to walk before he tried to run. He told him to live by three simple rules every time he stepped onto the hardwood: "Your ball, your court, your game! That was his credo, and he never lets me

Philip Harrison watches some March Madness with nephew Malcolm in what has become a Shaq shrine.

go back."

Like many fathers, Harrison was his son's first coach. He drilled Shaquille on the old Boston forget it," Shaquille says.

Obviously, he hasn't.

Shaq grew up wanting to play the game like his idol Dr. J, Julius Erving. He fondly remembers the time at LSU when Erving made a surprising house call while he was still asleep in his dorm room. "I woke up when Dr. J nudged me," O'Neal remembers. "I couldn't believe my eyes. I thought I was dreaming."

Today, many of tomorrow's superstars dream of meeting Shaq. At 23, he's already a role model for his generation. Realizing this, O'Neal takes it upon himself to communicate the "Stay in School" and "Say No To Drugs" messages to youngsters every chance he gets.

But while Shaq often uses what he's learned from his predecessors such as Dr. J and Michael Jordan, he always comes back to his one true role model — his dad — for guidance.

"My dad has always been my hero and my role model," Shaq says. "If it wasn't for my father, I wouldn't have the discipline I have now, and I wouldn't have the basketball skills I have now. I used to be lazy until my father kicked me in the rear end and got me going!"

He's been going full speed ever since.   •

— *Rudy J. Klancnik*

ford Smiths. Everyone wanted to see this phenom, but nobody wanted to play the tiny 2A school.

"In our non-district games, we tried to play as many 4A teams as we could," Madura says. "The 5A schools wouldn't touch us because it would have been too embarrassing to lose to a 2A school. I don't blame them. If I'd been a 5A coach, I wouldn't have played us, either."

At Liberty Hill, meanwhile, Segler didn't have much of a choice. The road to the state tournament went right through Cole and its 6-8 center. But by getting O'Neal into early foul trouble

— Segler took a timeout a minute into the game to change the strategy when O'Neal didn't come out guarding the Liberty Hill player Segler expected — Cole lost for the first and only time in the O'Neal era.

Of course, if you were to believe a certain hyperactive, bald-headed former coach who speaks his mind for ESPN, O'Neal's high school team was a perfect 69-0. That was what Dick Vitale said during a March Madness telecast in 1990, a telecast that those 1988 Liberty Hill players happened to see during a reunion at Segler's house to celebrate their Texas high school Final Four appearance.

"I practically had to scrape them off the wall," Segler recalls. "The kids went crazy, trying to call the TV station and everything. They had a lot of pride in what they did, and beating Shaquille O'Neal was part of it."

Cole and Liberty Hill, with new head coach Danny Henderson, met in the playoffs again in 1989. This time, O'Neal would not be stopped. He scored 44 points, and the Cougars won, 85-72, en route to a 36-0 championship season. Shaq's high school jersey (No. 33) was retired shortly after his final game. Henderson told Segler afterward, "You beat a child; we lost to a man."

"And he was right," Segler says. "The guy was all man."

Meanwhile, several hundred miles east of San Antonio on Interstate 10, LSU's Brown had maintained more than

a passing interest in O'Neal. It wasn't surprising then, when the blue-chip center decided to call Baton Rouge his college home.

LSU had produced its share of legends — Bob Pettit Jr. and Pete Maravich, to name a couple. But the Tigers, and college basketball, never had experienced anyone like Shaq.

Scouts called him a 7-foot Charles Barkley. Shaq was said to have David Robinson's quickness, Patrick Ewing's strength and Hakeem Olajuwon's agility.

If O'Neal had declared himself eligible for the draft after his freshman season, NBA experts say he would have been the first pick. They said the same thing after his sophomore season, when speculation surrounding his early departure grew to epic proportions. By the time O'Neal was in his third season, the NBA was on its knees begging the big guy to join them.

His nickname at LSU was Real Deal. O'Neal says he earned the tag because of his penchant for talking people into giving him deals on items he wanted to buy. But Real Deal fit for other reasons, as well.

In three years at LSU, O'Neal averaged 21.9 points and 13.6 rebounds, and in 1991 he became the only player

SHAQUILLE O'NEAL'S COLLEGIATE STATS

Season	Team	G	Min.	FG%	FT%	Reb.	Pts.	Avg.
'89-90	Louisiana State	32	901	.573	.556	385	445	13.9
'90-91	Louisiana State	28	881	.628	.638	411	774	27.6
'91-92	Louisiana State	30	959	.615	.528	421	722	24.1
	Totals	90	2,741	.610	.575	1,217	1,941	21.6

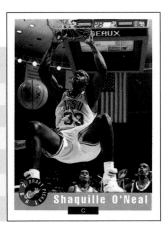

A group of guys from Liberty Hill, Texas, did something few college teams could and few NBA teams ever will: They repelled the Shaq Attack.

FOCUS ON SPORTS

in Southeastern Conference history to lead the league in scoring (27.6), rebounding (14.7), field-goal percentage (.628) and blocked shots (140) in one season.

Considering the undivided attention Shaq received every time he walked onto the floor, these individual accomplishments proved this kid was for real.

Yet for all the numbers and honors O'Neal accumulated, the Tigers never won more than 23 games in a season and captured the SEC regular season title only once, in O'Neal's sophomore year. They never won more than one NCAA tournament game. And Brown says failing to meet others' expectations, as unrealistic as they might have been, was the one drawback of coaching O'Neal.

"People don't take into account that Shaquille didn't have a great supporting cast around him. We weren't an especially good perimeter shooting team, so Shaquille often got buried by zones," says Brown, who was often outraged over the constant hacking Shaq had to endure. "But what I'll remember first and always about the O'Neal era at LSU is what an exceptional young man he was. He was just wonderful with my family. They adored him.

"Another thing that stood out about him was that even though every publication in the country was writing about him, he was first and always concerned about the team," Brown adds. "He always did a superb job of keeping his head on straight, and I credit that to his family. They brought him up right."

With his lyrical name and his dominating game, O'Neal seemed almost destined for greatness, even in his basketball infancy. And what he's done in his first three seasons with the NBA's Orlando Magic ensures he'll go down in history as one of the sport's greatest players.

Consequently, for those who saw him in the early days, the image always will remain vivid.

They marveled at him when he simply was the big kid from Cole, not yet the one-man conglomerate who was on the verge of being basketball's leading luminary. And that's why what occurred on March 5, 1988, never will be forgotten in the little central Texas town of Liberty Hill.

"I've got the tape of that game and I'm going to make copies for all my guys so someday they can show their kids the day they beat Shaq," Segler says. "That's a keeper for all time." •

Randy Riggs covers the NBA for the Austin *(Texas)* American-Statesman.

The BIG Picture

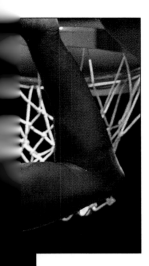

Up, UP and Away!

It's not a bird or a plane. It's Shaquille O'Neal, who's armed with much more than merely a tatoo of the Man of Steel. In street clothes, he's a mild-mannered young man thinking up new lyrics for his next rap release. But when he dons his favorite outfit, Shaq becomes faster than speeding All-Star centers, stops locomotive power forwards in their tracks and leaps point guards in a single bound. Shaq quickly picked up on the superhero motif by adding the Superman logo to the grille of his car.

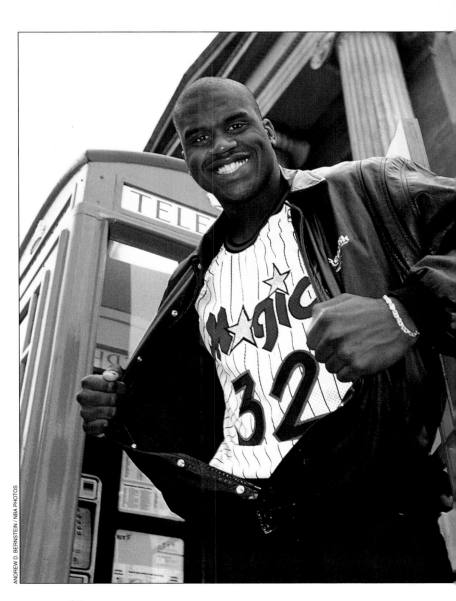

BOB ROSATO

TOM DIPACE

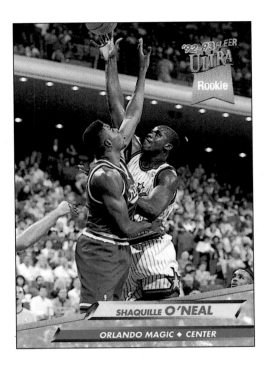

SHAQUILLE O'NEAL
ORLANDO MAGIC ◆ CENTER

His TURF

Not since The Big Dipper, Wilt Chamberlain, has the NBA seen a player with such an overpowering inside game. Once the ball moves to the low post, O'Neal becomes a man on a mission. And few are brave enough to stand in his way.

Calling
CARD

In 1991-92, Otis Thorpe led the NBA with 162 dunks. In '92-93, Shaq rattled the rim 322 times. Since the league started keeping track of slams in 1987-88, no player had even reached 200 in a season. Charles Barkley was the overall dunk king with 917 when the '93-94 season tipped off. It won't be long before that crown is passed along.

FERNANDO MEDINA / F. M. ASSOC.

FERNANDO MEDINA / F. M. ASSOC.

First Team · UPPER DECK™

Shaquille O'Neal · C

Shaq's KINGDOM

Disney World has nothing on the newest magic kingdom in Orlando, Shaq's 22,000-square foot lakeside mansion. It certainly is a neighborhood attraction, as the note and offering on his doorstep from a young fan attests. If anyone doesn't know who lives there, the license plate on the car in the driveway provides a telling clue.

The Many FACES of Shaq

An unending source of delight for photographers, Shaq cuts an interesting figure even when he may not be intending to. Whether he's popping out of a shirt, scrunching his face, smiling broadly or affecting the *caballero* look, O'Neal is a camera's best friend.

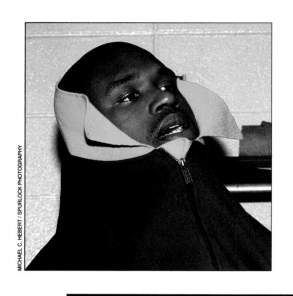

MICHAEL C. HEBERT / SPURLOCK PHOTOGRAPHY

MIKE COOPER / ALLSPORT USA

JOHN McDONOUGH / SPORTS ILLUSTRATED

BILL FRAKES / SPORTS ILLUSTRATED

Walt Disney World long has been the last word in family fun. But thanks to a

7-1, 303-pound attraction named Shaq, there's

A NEW MAGIC KINGDOM

By Bill Fay

O'Neal's 22 EEE's fit perfectly into Reebok's game plan, while Pepsi kept step with Coke by making the big guy the right one, baby . . . uh, huh.

Shaquille O'Neal says he's a basketball player, not an entertainer. Yet from Day One of his Orlando Magic career, he's stuck to the showman's creed: Give 'em what they want.

So when O'Neal emerged from an airplane June 25, 1992, the morning after the Magic made him the first pick in that year's draft, he wore a pair of mouse ears. Mickey Mouse ears.

"Tell Mickey he's got some company," Shaq said as the crowd of fans burst into laughter and applause. "Shaqie Mouse is now in town."

He no longer wears the mouse ears, but he's nearly as recognizable as the Disney icon around Central Florida. It may not be long before he's as well known as Mickey around the world, too.

O'Neal's Goliath size, backboard-shattering basketball skills and deft sense of where the camera is and how to smile into it have catapulted him onto center stage. He's toured Europe, Australia and the Orient. Africa and South America also found their ways onto Shaq's itinerary. Soon, the penguins at the

North and South Pole will be the only ones who haven't seen, heard or read about the famous Shaq.

"He is a multimedia, multicultural phenomenon," says his agent, Leonard Armato, who has crafted a good many of Shaq's multiple personas. "He's an icon, a 7-1, 300-pound entertainer who's instantly recognizable by several segments of society. There haven't been many people who have his talent, his charisma, his natural appeal."

Michael Jordan does. Only His Airness' return to the hardwood right before the playoffs this season could steal

The biggest mobile billboard money can buy, Shaq will go anywhere and do almost anything for a quality endorsement.

BARRY GOSSAGE PHOTOGRAPHY

the limelight away from the big man. Remember, Michael retired as the undisputed king of endorsements with an estimated $35 million a year in outside-basketball income. But it took even His Highness a few years of hang gliding before he was knocking 'em dead on Madison Avenue as successfully as he was at Madison Square Garden.

Shaq's star shot into orbit the minute he declared himself eligible for the NBA draft.

He was a national phenomenon while still at LSU, but couldn't make a dime in outside income because of archaic NCAA rules that forbid so much as a poster pose for a charity calendar. When he announced his decision to leave LSU after his junior year, he had a good idea of what to expect.

"I became a professional, and as a professional, you have to deal with me as a basketball player and a businessman," Shaq says, sounding out the "and" with emphasis.

The Magic discovered just what he meant soon after the 1992 draft. Shaq and Armato weren't just talking big numbers, they were talking about the richest contract of any player in organized sports.

They got it without much fuss.

The Magic agreed to pay Shaq $40 million for seven years, all of it guaranteed and some of it renegotiable. One clause in the contract allows Shaq to go back and ask for more after his

third season. He already has said he will exercise that clause at the appropriate time, but management isn't worried.

"Shaq has more than lived up to his end of the contract," Magic general manager Pat Williams says. "We had no idea he'd have this big an impact on our team and our city. He's raised the team to a level where we should be a playoff team for many years.

"And Orlando is reaping the benefits of his global exposure. You can go anywhere in the United States and see kids wearing Orlando Magic hats, shirts

or whatever. And that same thing is happening all over the world now because of Shaq."

The initial reaction to Shaq in Orlando, a tourist town where a good many people work in service-industry jobs, was split. A few said he was worth every penny. Most wondered how any 20-year-old, regardless of his basketball skills, could be worth that kind of dough. The doubters became converts a week into the regular season.

O'Neal exploded out of the blocks,

After his rookie season, Shaq ranked sixth on *Forbes* magazine's list of the world 40 highest-paid sports stars. Today, he's closing in on the top spot.

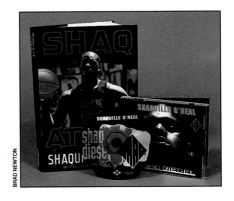

averaging 25.0 points, 16.8 rebounds and 3.5 blocks while shooting 57.3 percent from the field that first week. He's the only rookie in NBA history to win the league's Player of the Week Award in his first week as a pro. By the time Shaq became the 14th rookie starter in the All-Star Game — he received more than 800,000 votes — everyone in Orlando and the NBA was convinced they were watching something special.

Magic fans quickly realized — as Shaq had suggested his first day in Or-lando — that they weren't living in a Mickey Mouse town anymore. O'Neal's talent was going to propel the Magic, and Orlando along with it, into the national spotlight.

Corporate America had a quicker vision of the future. Reebok, once the sports footwear of choice in the United States but a company reeling from the popularity of Jordan and his Nike en-dorsements, jumped on Shaq's band-wagon before he even signed with the Magic.

The shoe company gave him a five-year, $15 million endorsement deal in the summer of 1992, then tore that up a year later and upped the ante to $20 million across four years.

"We needed someone who could elevate the perception of the brand as well as help us with the sales end of it, and Shaq was the man," Reebok spokesman Dave Fogelson says. "He's what we call a halo effect for Reebok. It really improves our image when athletes in other sports see Shaq posi-tioned with Reebok. He's sort of the center piece to a big puzzle we're

The rap on Shaq is that he spends too much of his summer working on his skills away from the court. But NBA centers are humming a different tune.

NATHANIEL S. BUTLER / NBA PHOTOS

putting together that includes football and basketball players. They gain confidence in us when they see what we've done with Shaq."

Shaq says he chose to go with Reebok instead of powerhouse Nike when the Nike people failed to make him feel wanted. "They told me they were going to put my name on a shoe along with Charles Barkley and some others," O'Neal writes in his autobiography, *Shaq Attaq!* "That's the phrase that stuck with me — 'along with.' "

About the same time he was slipping on his new shoes, Shaq was signing an exclusive two-year, $2.5 million deal with Classic Games, makers of draft picks card sets. Even if he hadn't signed with the Magic, O'Neal was financially set for some time.

Spalding was next, unveiling its line of Shaq autographed basketballs in December 1992. Sales of the ball exceeded projections by 25 percent, reports Spalding marketing director John Doleva. "And we set very aggressive goals," Doleva says. "The success with the Shaq ball has been phenomenal. He's as close to a guaranteed performer as you're going to get. We needed a franchise player who'd be around a while, and we've got it."

Pepsi won a spirited battle with Coca-Cola to become Shaq's official soft drink and probably has done the most creative work in marketing him. O'Neal says the "Don't Even Think About It" ad with the adorable little boy is his favorite commercial spot.

Then along came rap. A performance with the group Fu Schnickens on *The Arsenio Hall Show*. A gig at the NBA All-Star Weekend. A recording contract with Jive Records. The release of his first album, *Shaq Diesel*, which shipped gold.

"There are a lot of skeptics out there who think we only signed him because of his name," Jive Records senior vice president and general manager Barry Weiss says. "Well, I'm here to tell you, Shaq has as much talent in a recording studio as he does on a basketball court. He's going to be a major force in rap music."

All of a sudden, he's not just a basketball player and major endorser, he's a force in the music world. A whole segment of society is tuning in and turning on to Shaq.

That's great for the Magic, the NBA, the companies O'Neal endorses

Shaq's appeal to the MTV generation is evident at every turn. Just think how popular he could become if he brings the Magic a world title or two.

and his music label. But is there a chance we'll all become Shaq-saturated and tire of him?

"There is such a thing as over-exposure," says Armato, who is paid to make sure it doesn't happen. "But we've selected the products, the number of appearances and whatever else we can control to guard against it.

"The big thing we're after is quality, not quantity. We want to make sure everything Shaq does is creative and credible. He's obviously proven he's credible in basketball. The album proves he's credible in music. We're not going to put him into a medium where he embarrasses himself."

Shaq's attitude also proves that he's in this for the long haul.

"The one thing that I think hurt Michael [Jordan] over the years was that his commercials built him up to be some kind of superhero," O'Neal says. "He became bigger than life. I didn't want that to happen to me, and I thought a long time about it before agreeing to my commercial deals, In the Pepsi ad, I bring down the rim to dunk without leaving the ground, but then get dissed by a little kid. In the Reebok ad with the NBA greats, I break a backboard, but then have to clean up the glass. I want people to know I'm a real person."

For the next, oh, decade or so, the world will get to know Shaq and his Magic Kingdom very well. •

Bill Fay covers the Magic for The Tampa Tribune.

By Pete Williams

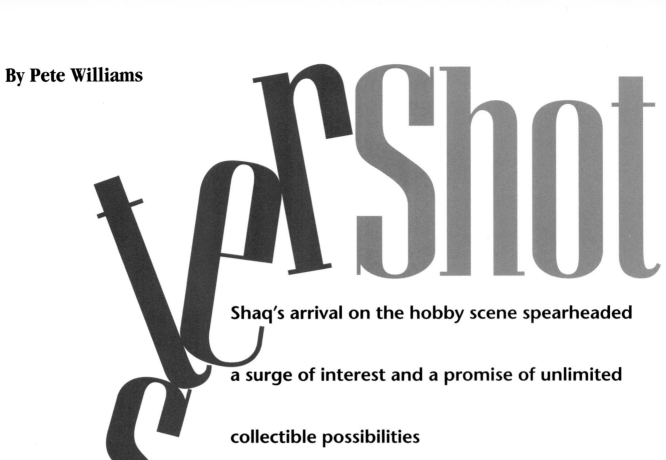

OverShot

Shaq's arrival on the hobby scene spearheaded

a surge of interest and a promise of unlimited

collectible possibilities

On the eve of the 1992 National Sports Collectors Convention, a white stretch limousine pulled up to the Atlanta Marriott Marquis. Prominently displaying the familiar green logo of Classic Games on its doors, the vehicle could have contained any one of the athletes arriving to sign autographs at the show.

But this was no ordinary limo, because it contained no ordinary athlete. Out stepped Shaquille O'Neal.

Two weeks earlier, the Orlando Magic made Shaq the top prize at the NBA draft. Now this 7-1 man-child would make a similar impact on the hobby at the Georgia World Congress Center.

The industry hasn't been the same since.

In just three NBA seasons, Shaquille has

emerged as the most marketable athlete this side of His Airness, Michael Jordan. In fact, Shaq's product endorsements, especially with Reebok and Pepsi, have turned Shaq into a household name. Score Board, the parent company of Classic, hopes to take it further after signing O'Neal to a five-year, multimillion dollar deal in November for exclusive rights to a wide range of products.

Shaq is everywhere. And anything associated with Shaq prospers. Certainly, no industry has reaped the rewards more than the sports card and memorabilia business.

Even in a field as competitive as sports card collecting, Shaq has become a dominant force. Many hobby dealers credit O'Neal with saving their

BRAD NEWTON

shops. And while baseball offers superstars Frank Thomas and Juan Gonzalez, Shaq's popularity extends even further. He single-handedly silenced most of the gloom-and-doom prognosticators who predicted an industry crash.

"He kept the business alive," points out Gary Nagle, whose Baseball Card Works in Kissimmee, Fla., is just a half hour from Orlando. "Baseball and football cards weren't selling. If it weren't for Shaq, a lot of people wouldn't have sold anything."

Not surprisingly, when lists are compiled of the most influential people in the hobby, Shaq usually ranks at or near the top.

"Last year, all anybody wanted was Shaq," says Joe Bosley of The Old Ball Game in Teisterstown, Md. "I've never seen anything like it. It was like nothing else mattered."

Seven years ago, card manufacturers considered basketball an afterthought. Fleer signed up as the only company to obtain an NBA license. Sure, the stars were in place: Michael Jordan, Magic Johnson and Larry Bird. But baseball still reigned as the undisputed hobby heavyweight.

Since that time, however, baseball's popularity has been slipping, particularly among the nation's youth. Basketball, thanks to the NBA's superior marketing job, filled the gap. And then Shaq arrived in 1992, the natural successor to Jordan, Magic and Bird.

Finally, NBA cards were beginning to rival those of baseball.

Sets seemingly multiplied in 1992-93, each offering a Hot Shaq card — and yet collectors still couldn't get enough. O'Neal's Stadium Club Beam Team insert (#21) became the Hottest card in the hobby through the winter and spring of 1993. Other cards, such as Hoops Draft Redemption (#A), SkyBox

Draft Picks (#1) and Hoops Magic's All-Rookie Team insert (#1) boosted hobby interest to a frenzy, with a dozen other Rookie Cards almost as hard to pull.

For a while, it appeared that only Classic would boast a line of O'Neal RCs. By signing Shaq to an exclusive card contract through Dec. 31, 1992, Classic guaranteed itself the only O'Neal card on the market until New Year's Day.

Other card companies were furious. Yet there was nothing they could do, since O'Neal had signed the contract before he inked a deal with the Magic and automatically became included in the NBA's group licensing program. Without a license from the NBA to produce cards, Classic was free to cut its own deal, and outbid all competitors.

"It was worth the extra money to have him tied to us," said Ken

Classic wrapped up Shaq until Jan. 1, 1993, but NBA licensees quickly made up for lost time. The big winner was 1992-93 Beam Team (#21), which is considered one of his top mainstream issues.

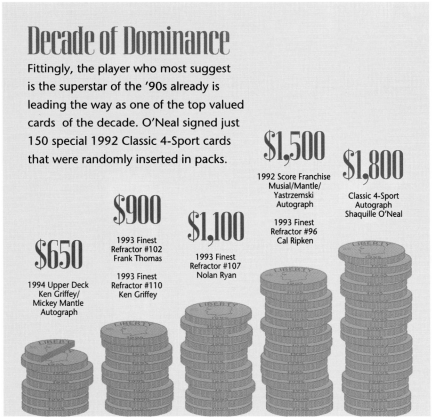

Decade of Dominance

Fittingly, the player who most suggest is the superstar of the '90s already is leading the way as one of the top valued cards of the decade. O'Neal signed just 150 special 1992 Classic 4-Sport cards that were randomly inserted in packs.

$650
1994 Upper Deck Ken Griffey/ Mickey Mantle Autograph

$900
1993 Finest Refractor #102 Frank Thomas

1993 Finest Refractor #110 Ken Griffey

$1,100
1993 Finest Refractor #107 Nolan Ryan

$1,500
1992 Score Franchise Musial/Mantle/ Yastrzemski Autograph

1993 Finest Refractor #96 Cal Ripken

$1,800
Classic 4-Sport Autograph Shaquille O'Neal

All values are taken from various issues of Beckett® Price Guides.

Pushed by Classic to their creative limits, Hoops and Upper Deck struck gold with their redemption and trade card ideas. Series II sets that included Shaq inserts also became mega hits with collectors.

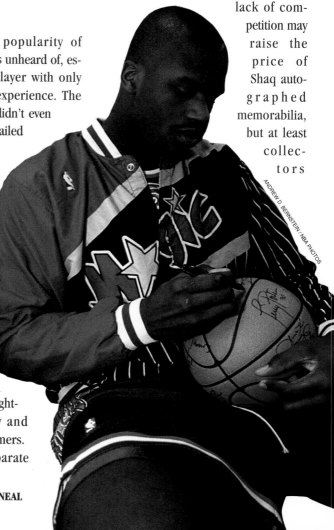

Goldin, executive vice president of Score Board Inc., the parent company of Classic. "We knew that having him exclusively would give us a huge marketing advantage."

Even though the other companies balked, the Classic exclusive probably helped everybody in the long run. Classic owned the hobby's brightest new face, and the other manufacturers had three months longer than usual to hype their cards. Even O'Neal redemption cards, thinly veiled as "trade" cards, became Hot collectibles.

Because of Shaq's exclusive deal with Classic — and similar exclusives the company signed with 1993 lottery picks Chris Webber and Anfernee Hardaway — the "trade" card no longer is viewed as a novelty, but has become a regular and accepted part of the basketball card hobby. The practice also branched out to hockey, as Score offered collectors a redemption card for No. 1 draft pick

Alexandre Daigle's first NHL issue.

Classic scooped the other companies, but some collectors argue that Classic's four O'Neal cards can't claim an RC title since Shaq isn't shown in a Magic uniform. Only league-licensed cards are used to determine RCs, and Classic Shaq cards were not licensed by the NBA. Among the many O'Neal RCs, the one with the most staying power might be his Beam Team card, which climbed to as much as $300 after its release. How ironic that Topps issued that Hot commodity, since the company had given up on basketball cards in the early 1980s and scrambled to reacquire a license for 1992.

The price and popularity of O'Neal cards was unheard of, especially for a player with only one season of experience. The Orlando Magic didn't even finish above .500 and failed to make the playoffs.

But Shaq's charisma, along with the aggressive management style of agent/manager Leonard Armato, captured the attention of the sports collecting hobby.

Advertising deals with Reebok, Pepsi and Spalding heightened Shaq's visibility and recognition with consumers. Armato even cut a separate

deal with Kenner to market Starting Lineup action figures — a $6 retail item that promptly traded for as much as $50 in some secondary market circles upon their release.

Score Board's November agreement with Shaq not only includes exclusive autograph rights, but also corporate sponsorship. Hallmark will be introducing a line of Shaq gift wrap and greeting cards, and MBNA America, the largest credit card bank in the United States, also will produce collectible items. Is a Shaq charge card in the near future?

"We feel he is the dominant sports figure, not only in basketball, but in the world in any sport," Goldin says.

Although Shaq still can sign autographs for free or for charity purposes, the Score Board deal limits his signature on licensed collectibles to Score Board products. The lack of competition may raise the price of Shaq autographed memorabilia, but at least collectors

ANDREW D. BERNSTEIN / NBA PHOTOS

By inking the game's biggest name to an exclusive contract, Classic added a new catchphrase — redemption cards — to the hobby's vocabulary

Classic Shaq

By Theo Chen

Of the countless autographs Shaquille O'Neal has penned since his emergence as an NBA megastar, the most significant to the hobby was his signature at the bottom of an exclusive contract for Classic Games in 1992.

This agreement prevented Shaq from appearing on NBA-licensed cards until Jan. 1, 1993. As a result, Shaq's Classic cards became the only game in town at the start of his rookie season. When O'Neal caught fire as the league's newest sensation, so did those cards.

Quick Ascent

Even now, after Shaq's appearances on a boatload of NBA cards, seven of his Classic cards — autographed special cards, inserts and one autographed insert at the very top — rank among his 10 most valuable mainstream cards.

Where did it start? With the basketball previews randomly inserted in the Classic Football Draft Picks packs. Just 10,000 five-card sets were inserted, and Shaq's preview card soon shot up to triple-digit prices.

The regular 1992 Classic basketball arrived next. To no one's surprise, that set became the most successful draft picks set produced. Shaq's regular (#1) and LP (#LP1) cards were red-Hot for months. The gold-foil stamped version of the set, produced months later only in factory set form, contained a specially signed, individually numbered Shaq card in each set.

Following Classic basketball was the company's baseball and hockey sets, featuring random insert Four-Sport previews, including Shaq (#CC1).

The Four-Sport packs rivaled Classic basketball, thanks in no small part to the full-bleed LP insert set containing a Shaq (#LP8),

a Shaq/Kareem Abdul-Jabbar combo (#LP14) and a Future Superstars card (#LP15) with Shaq and fellow first overall picks.

This Future Superstars card was adapted as a random insert in Four-Sport jumbo packs (#FS1). An autographed version came one per set in the Four-Sport gold-foil stamped factory sets, released in mid-1993.

The king of the Shaq cards, however, can be found in regular 1992 Classic Four-Sport packs. It's the Shaq autograph card, individually numbered out of 150 and currently valued at $1,200-$1,800. Not surprisingly, counterfeit versions have infiltrated the market.

Aside from that monumental card, interest in Classic Shaq cards has faded somewhat with so many NBA cards available. Even so, Classic did include him in its 1993 basketball draft picks as a Flashback in the regular set (#104) and in the LP insert set (#LP9).

Another 1993 Classic Shaq card is considered borderline mainstream. He appears on card #28 in the 1993 Four-Sport McDonald's regional set distributed in parts of Pennsylvania and Florida. The McDonald's cards were packaged in five-card foil packs sold last fall.

Mood Swing

Most hobbyists predicted that Shaq's exclusive contract would not only upset the NBA's licensed card manufacturers, but actually take money out of their pockets.

That prediction, however, proved only 50 percent correct. Shaq's delayed entry into the NBA card arena likely helped, not hindered, the finances of the NBA-licensed manufacturers.

To deal with this unique situation, Hoops and Upper Deck created Redemption and Trade cards, respectively, for their Series I products. Both concepts worked well. The Hoops Redemption card, in particular, worked better in the long run because of its scarcity, early redemption deadline and special redemption set, which included not only a Shaq card, but all lottery picks who had signed NBA contracts prior to a specific date.

Despite the popularity of these trade-in and Classic Shaq cards, demand for O'Neal cardboard wasn't even close to satisfied. Classic and trade-in cards merely whetted collectors' appetites for the main course of Series II NBA cards.

As a result, the various Series II products became the most eagerly awaited basketball cards ever.

In hindsight, tremendous irony exists with Shaq's Classic exclusive contract. Obviously, the agreement made 1992 and 1993 blockbuster years for Classic. But instead of dealing a serious blow to the licensed-NBA card market, Classic actually helped fuel the ShaqMania contributing to the market's amazing growth. •

Theo Chen is a Price Guide analyst for Beckett Publications.

know the items they get from Score Board are legitimate.

In addition, all of Shaq's non-NBA licensed cards will be handled by Classic, a subsidiary of Score Board. Classic will produce a line of Shaq collectibles, including coins, silver and bronze cards, and ceramic cards, plates and figurines. Classic's first television marketing campaign also will use Shaq as its spokesman.

Other endorsement deals have spawned dozens of paper collectible Shaq products, including Pepsi and Reebok cardboard standups, along with the largest number of posters not portraying a guy named Jordan. O'Neal's childlike qualities, his massive dunks and his talent for tearing down rims all help create the Shaq mystique.

He couldn't have picked a better time.

"With Michael, Magic and Bird gone," says Michigan-based dealer Michael Lupo, "[O'Neal] has the potential to dominate the field."

Many of the NBA's previous big men portrayed themselves as meanspirited players — and that hurt their marketability. When Wilt Chamberlain was asked to explain his bad-guy image, he replied, "Nobody likes Goliath."

Bill Russell and Kareem Abdul-Jabbar both appeared aloof. Patrick Ewing constantly wears a menacing glower. Even future star Alonzo Mourning plays with a perpetual scowl.

But O'Neal has captured the hearts of millions with his smile and humor. He cultivates the reputation of a gentle giant — even more so than San Antonio's David Robinson, a hobby hero just five years ago.

"There really has never been as popular a big man," notes Eric Clements of Eric's Baseball Cards in Titusville, Fla. "[But Shaq's] personality and size have made him unique among athletes. Collectors appreciate that."

Duane Garrett, of Richard Wolffers Auctions, says Shaq has a Ruthian quality — a player who is larger than life.

"People are attracted to the prodigious feats," says Garrett, whose firm sold an O'Neal game-worn jersey for $8,800. "Some guys shatter backboards. Shaq brings down the entire

Adding a game-worn O'Neal jersey to your collection takes some serious sweat — and plenty of cash.

BRAD NEWTON / COURTESY OF JORDAN'S SPORTSCARDS IN ORLANDO

goal. That's where the popularity comes from. Stopping the game by destroying the stadium is the ultimate in sports. It's like Roy Hobbs in *The Natural* taking out the lights."

O'Neal's game-worn jerseys have become the centerpiece of sports auctions. While $8,800 for the jersey at Wolffers was considered high, nothing compares to the $55,000 paid for Shaq's first NBA All-Star jersey at an auction held in conjunction with the 1992-93 All-Star Game in Salt Lake City.

The buyer? None other than Upper Deck CEO Richard McWilliam.

"He's just a huge, huge collector," Upper Deck spokesman Richard Bradley says of his boss. "It was

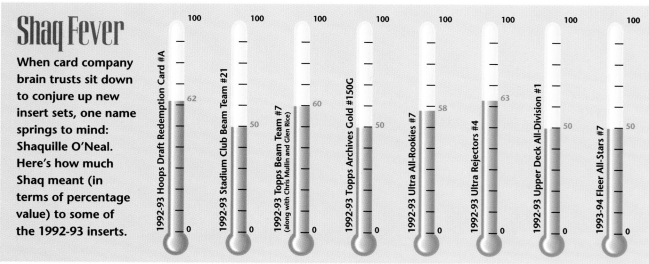

Shaq Fever

When card company brain trusts sit down to conjure up new insert sets, one name springs to mind: Shaquille O'Neal. Here's how much Shaq meant (in terms of percentage value) to some of the 1992-93 inserts.

1992-93 Hoops Draft Redemption Card #A — 62
1992-93 Stadium Club Beam Team #21 — 50
1992-93 Topps Beam Team #7 (along with Chris Mullin and Glen Rice) — 60
1992-93 Topps Archives Gold #150G — 50
1992-93 Ultra All-Rookies #7 — 58
1992-93 Ultra Rejectors #4 — 63
1992-93 Upper Deck All-Division #1 — 50
1993-94 Fleer All-Stars #7 — 50

*Note: Shaq is the highest valued card in each set. All prices are taken from the December 1993 issue of Beckett Basketball Monthly.

Shaq's first All-Star jersey, a game-worn jersey. There will never be another one."

Like an increasing number of athletes, O'Neal insists on personalizing autographs. That way, he figures to deter those people out to resell his autograph, while at the same time adding a special touch to the signature.

In his autobiography, *Shaq Attaq*, O'Neal reveals some of his problems with overzealous signature seekers.

"What makes me mad is when you go to a city and see the same people getting stuff signed over and over," he writes. "They're trying to insult my intelligence — like I don't know they're trying to make money off my name.

"I wish I didn't have to have this attitude about autographs. I wish autographs were for little kids to take home, sleep with at night, or put up on their wall in a nice frame. But they're not. Many of them are for adults, for profit. And that's a shame."

To promote the book, O'Neal appeared at a number of Orlando-area bookstores, where collectors got in line as early as 4 a.m. for 10 a.m. arrivals. Autographed copies of the 23-year-old's book have sold for as much as $150.

The Magic bolstered its public relations staff, in part to process the massive number of autograph requests coming through the team offices. The networks televising NBA games have increased the Magic's appearances from seven in 1992-93 to 17 in 1993-94 in order to feed off Shaq's popularity.

Whether Shaq was wearing a suit for a cheesy draft-day shot or just showing up on another player's card, he was the headline performer in '92-93. Bill Cartwright's card actually garners hobby attention because No. 32 appears with him.

As O'Neal becomes even more of a pop icon, with the ability to transcend sport, his fame in the hobby still may experience its ups and downs. At the end of the 1992-93 season, collectors already seemed tired of all the Shaq hype, especially when he was compared to Charlotte center Mourning.

Yet unless O'Neal has a disastrous season or is felled by injury, his hobby interest should never really nosedive. The odds are better that Shaq will remain a collector favorite for a long time.

Consider this: In 1992, the Georgia World Congress Center, site of that year's National, hosted the "Supershow" sporting goods convention. A towering cutout of O'Neal loomed three stories above the show floor. Looking up into the sky, an observer wondered if the cardboard O'Neal was a life-size reproduction.

As far as the hobby is concerned, it might have been constructed below scale. •

Pete Williams writes a collectibles column for USA Today.

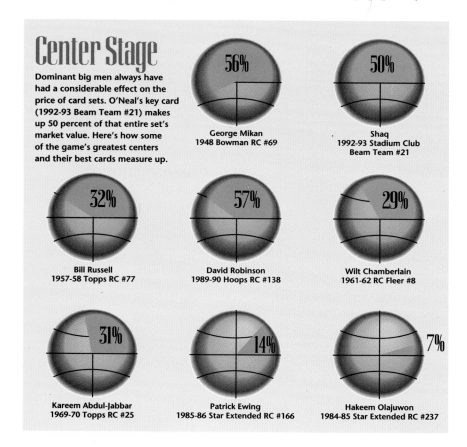

Center Stage

Dominant big men always have had a considerable effect on the price of card sets. O'Neal's key card (1992-93 Beam Team #21) makes up 50 percent of that entire set's market value. Here's how some of the game's greatest centers and their best cards measure up.

56%
George Mikan
1948 Bowman RC #69

50%
Shaq
1992-93 Stadium Club
Beam Team #21

32%
Bill Russell
1957-58 Topps RC #77

57%
David Robinson
1989-90 Hoops RC #138

29%
Wilt Chamberlain
1961-62 RC Fleer #8

31%
Kareem Abdul-Jabbar
1969-70 Topps RC #25

14%
Patrick Ewing
1985-86 Star Extended RC #166

7%
Hakeem Olajuwon
1984-85 Star Extended RC #237

Shaquille O'Neal's
Comprehensive
Card Checklist and Price Guide

- ❏ '90-91 Kentucky Big Blue Dream Team/Award Winners #19 $25-50
- ❏ '92 Classic Four-Sport* #1 $2-4
- ❏ '92 Classic Four-Sport* #318 John Wooden Award .75-$2
- ❏ '92 Classic Four-Sport Autograph* #1A $1400-1800
- ❏ '92 Classic Four-Sport Gold* #1 $12-24
- ❏ '92 Classic Four-Sport Gold* #318 John Wooden Award $6-12
- ❏ '92 Classic Four-Sport Gold* #AU Multiplayer $50-75
- ❏ '92 Classic Four-Sport BC* #FS1 Multiplayer $25-40
- ❏ '92 Classic Four-Sport LP* #LP14 Multiplayer $7.50-15
- ❏ '92 Classic Four-Sport LP* #LP15 Multiplayer $7.50-15
- ❏ '92 Classic Four-Sport LP* #LP8 $20-40
- ❏ '92 Classic Four-Sport Preview* #CC1 $30-50
- ❏ '92 Classic Four-Sport Promos* #PR1 $15-30
- ❏ '92 Classic BK Previews #1 $65-100
- ❏ '92 Classic Draft Picks #1 $2.50-5
- ❏ '92 Classic Draft Picks Gold #1 $15-30
- ❏ '92 Classic Draft Picks Gold #AU $100-175
- ❏ '92 Classic Draft Picks LP #LP1 $20-40
- ❏ '92 Classic Draft Picks Promo #1 $20-40

- ❏ '92 Classic Show Promos 20* #11 $15-30
- ❏ '92 Classic Show Promos 20* #17 $15-30
- ❏ '92-93 Fleer #298 Slam Dunk $1-2.50
- ❏ '92-93 Fleer #401 $4-8
- ❏ '92-93 Fleer Drake #37 $6-12
- ❏ '92-93 Fleer Team Night Sheets #9 Multiplayer $5-10
- ❏ '92-93 Fleer Tony's Pizza #97 Slam Dunk $7.50-15
- ❏ '92-93 Hoops #442 $7-12
- ❏ '92-93 Hoops Draft Redemption #A $55-80
- ❏ '92-93 Hoops Magic's All-Rookies #1 $100-150
- ❏ '92-93 Panini Sticker #1 $4-8
- ❏ '92-93 SkyBox #382 $7-12
- ❏ '92-93 SkyBox Head of the Class #NNO Multiplayer $20-40
- ❏ '92-93 SkyBox Draft Picks #1 $25-40
- ❏ '92-93 Sports Illustrated for Kids #131 $2.50-5
- ❏ '92-93 Stadium Club #201 Members Choice $2.50-5
- ❏ '92-93 Stadium Club #247 $9-15
- ❏ '92-93 Stadium Club Beam Team #21 $90-120
- ❏ '92-93 Stadium Club Members Only #201 Members Choice $4-8
- ❏ '92-93 Stadium Club Members Only #247 $15-25
- ❏ '92-93 Stadium Club Members Only Beam Team #21 $35-60
- ❏ '92-93 Topps #362 $2-4
- ❏ '92-93 Topps Archives Gold #150 $12-20
- ❏ '92-93 Topps Beam Team #7 Multiplayer $1.50-3
- ❏ '92-93 Topps Beam Team Gold #7 Multiplayer $6-12
- ❏ '92-93 Topps Gold #362 $10-20
- ❏ '92-93 Ultra #328 $4-8
- ❏ '92-93 Ultra All-Rookies #7 $12-20
- ❏ '92-93 Ultra Rejectors #4 $10-20
- ❏ '92-93 Upper Deck #1B $4-8
- ❏ '92-93 Upper Deck #1 SP $9-15
- ❏ '92-93 Upper Deck #424 All-Star $1-2.50
- ❏ '92-93 Upper Deck #474 Top Prospect $1-2.50

- ❏ '92-93 Upper Deck All-Division #AD1 $6-12
- ❏ '92-93 Upper Deck MVP Holograms #35 $4-8
- ❏ '92-93 Upper Deck McDonald's #OR5 $7.50-15
- ❏ '92-93 Upper Deck McDonald's #P43 $3-6
- ❏ '92-93 Upper Deck Rookie Standouts #RS15 $9-15
- ❏ '92-93 Upper Deck Sheets #10 Multiplayer $10-20
- ❏ '93 Classic Four-Sport #315 All Rookie Team .25-.60
- ❏ '93 Classic Four-Sport Autograph #315 $325-450
- ❏ '93 Classic Four-Sport LPs #LP6 $2-4
- ❏ '93 Classic Four-Sport Tri-Cards #TC1 Multiplayer $5-10
- ❏ '93 Classic Four-Sport Gold #315 All Rookie Team $2-3.50
- ❏ '93 Classic Draft Tonx* #1 .50-$1
- ❏ '93 Classic Draft Tonx* #2 .50-$1

'92-93 Upper Deck #1B

- ❏ '93 Classic Draft Tonx* #3 .50-$1
- ❏ '93 Classic Draft Tonx* #4 .50-$1
- ❏ '93 Classic Draft Tonx* #5 .50-$1
- ❏ '93 Classic Draft Tonx* #6 .50-$1
- ❏ '93 Classic Draft Tonx Promos #PR1 $1.25-2.50
- ❏ '93 Classic Draft Tonx Collecting Club Promo* #PR1 $1.25-2.50
- ❏ '93 Classic Draft Special Bonus #SB20 $1.50-3
- ❏ '93 Classic Draft Gold #104 Flashback $1.25-2.50
- ❏ '93 Classic Draft LP #LP9 Flashback $3-6
- ❏ '93 Classic Draft Picks #104 Flashback .25-.60
- ❏ '93 Classic Draft Picks Draft Day #7 $4-8
- ❏ '93 Classic Collecting Club Draft Tonx* #1 .50-$1
- ❏ '93 Classic Collecting Club

- ❏ Draft Tonx* #2 .50 $1
- ❏ '93 Classic Collecting Club Draft Tonx* #3 .50-$1
- ❏ '93 Classic Collecting Club Draft Tonx* #4 .50-$1
- ❏ '93 Classic Collecting Club Draft Tonx* #5 .50-$1
- ❏ '93 Classic Collecting Club Draft Tonx* #6 .50-$1
- ❏ '93 Classic Futures #NNO Acetate $45-75
- ❏ '93 Classic McDonald's Four-Sport* #28 .75-$1.50
- ❏ '93 Classic Superheroes* #SS1 $5-10
- ❏ '93-94 Costacos Brothers Poster Cards* #15 $1.50-3
- ❏ '93-94 Fleer #149 .75-$1.75
- ❏ '93-94 Fleer #231 Award Winner .35-.90
- ❏ '93-94 Fleer All-Stars #7 $12-20
- ❏ '93-94 Fleer Rookie Sensations #18 $15-25
- ❏ '93-94 Fleer NBA Superstars #16 $3-6
- ❏ '93-94 Fleer Towers of Powers #21 $12.50-25
- ❏ '93 Fax Pax World of Sport* #8 $1.25-2.50
- ❏ '93-94 Finest #3 $7.50-15
- ❏ '93-94 Finest #99 Atlantic Finest $4.50-9
- ❏ '93-94 Finest Main Attraction #19 $25-40
- ❏ '93-94 Finest Refractors #3 $90-150
- ❏ '93-94 Finest Refractors #99 Atlantic Finest $45-75
- ❏ '93-94 Hoops Prototypes #6 $1.50-3
- ❏ '93-94 Hoops #155 .75-$1.75
- ❏ '93-94 Hoops #264 All-Stars .35-.90
- ❏ '93-94 Hoops #284 League Leader Multiplayer .10-.30
- ❏ '93-94 Hoops #290 League Leader Multiplayer .10-.30
- ❏ '93-94 Hoops Fifth Anniversary Gold #155 $2.50-5
- ❏ '93-94 Hoops Fifth Anniversary Gold #264 All-Star $1.50-3
- ❏ '93-94 Hoops Fifth Anniversary Gold #284 League Leader Multiplayer .50-$1
- ❏ '93-94 Hoops Fifth Anniversary Gold #290 League Leader Multiplayer .50-$1
- ❏ '93-94 Hoops Admiral's Choice #AC4 $1.25-2.50
- ❏ '93-94 Hoops Face to Face #1 Multiplayer $5-10
- ❏ '93-94 Hoops Supreme Court #SC4 $1.75-3.50
- ❏ '93-94 Hoops Team Sheet #6 Multiplayer $1.50-3
- ❏ '93-94 Jam Session #160 $1.50-3
- ❏ '93-94 Jam Session Second Year Stars #7 $2.50-5
- ❏ '93-94 Jam Session Slam

'92-93 Stadium Club Beam Team #21

Dunk Heroes #7 $2.50-5

❏ '93-94 Kenner Starting
Lineup (package) #20 $25-40

❏ '93-94 Panini Stickers #187 $2-4

❏ '93-94 Panini Stickers #C
Rookie of the Year $2-4

❏ '93-94 SkyBox #133 $1-2

❏ '93-94 SkyBox #331
Poster Card   .40-$1

❏ '93-94 SkyBox All-Rookies
#AR1 $12-20

❏ '93-94 SkyBox Center
Stage #CS2 $7.50-15

❏ '93-94 SkyBox Pepsi
Shaq Attaq set $15-25

❏ '93-94 SkyBox Promos #5
   $2.50-5

❏ '93-94 SkyBox Schick #36
   $6-12

❏ '93-94 SkyBox Shaq Talk set
   $25-40

❏ '93-94 SkyBox Showdown
Series #SS2 Multiplayer .60-$1.50

❏ '93-94 SkyBox Showdown
Series #SS3 Multiplayer .60-$1.50

❏ '93-94 SkyBox Thunder
and Lightning #TL6
Multiplayer $12-20

❏ '93-94 SkyBox USA Tip-Off
#10 Mulitplayer $5-10

❏ '93-94 Stadium Club
#100 $1.75-3.50

❏ '93-94 Stadium Club
#175 High Court   .75-$1.75

❏ '93-94 Stadium Club #358
Frequent Flyer   .40-$1

❏ '93-94 Stadium Club
First Day Issue #100 $60-120

❏ '93-94 Stadium Club First Day
Issue #175 High Court $30-60

❏ '93-94 Stadium Club First
Day Issue #358 Frequent
Flyer $30-60

❏ '93-94 Stadium Club
Beam Team #1 $15-25

❏ '93-94 Stadium Club Frequent
Flyer Point Cards #NNO $.40-$1
price each (5 different point totals)

❏ '93-94 Stadium Club Frequent
Flyer Upgrades #358 $12.50-25

❏ '93-94 Stadium Club Rim
Rockers #1 $5-10

'93-94 Finest #3

❏ '93-94 Stadium Club
Super Teams #19 $6-12

❏ '93-94 Stadium Club Super
Teams NBA Finals #100 $3.50-7

❏ '93-94 Stadium Club Super
Teams NBA Finals #175
High Court $1.75-3.50

❏ '93-94 Stadium Club Super
Teams NBA Finals #358
Frequent Flyer $2.50-5

'93-94 Hoops #155

❏ '93 Stadium Club Members
Only #NNO $2-4

❏ '93-94 Topps #134 All-Star
   .35-.90

❏ '93-94 Topps #152 All-
Rookie Team   .35-.90

❏ '93-94 Topps #181   .75-$1.75

❏ '93-94 Topps #386 Future
Scoring Leader   .35-.90

❏ '93-94 Topps #3 Highlight
   .35-.90

❏ '93-94 Topps Black Gold
#18 $4-8

❏ '93-94 Topps Gold
#134 All-Stars $1.75-3.50

❏ '93-94 Topps Gold #152
All Rookie Team $1.75-3.50

❏ '93-94 Topps Gold #181
   $3.75-7.50

❏ '93-94 Topps Gold #386
Future Scoring Leader $1.75-3.50

❏ '93-94 Topps Gold #3
Highlight $1.75-3.50

❏ '93-94 Ultra #135 $1-2

❏ '93-94 Ultra #M2 USA $2.50-5

❏ '93-94 Ultra All-Rookie
Team #5 $5-10

❏ '93-94 Ultra Award
Winners #4 $12-20

❏ '93-94 Ultra Jam City #7 $45-75

❏ '93-94 Ultra Famous
Nicknames #13 $4.50-9

❏ '93-94 Ultra Power
in the Key #7 $12-20

❏ '93-94 Ultra Rebound
Kings #9 $2.50-5

❏ '93-94 Ultra Scoring
Kings #8 $35-60

❏ '93-94 Upper Deck #177
Season Leaders   .40-$1

❏ '93-94 Upper Deck #228
Multiplayer   .20-.50

❏ '93-94 Upper Deck #300 $1-2

❏ '93-94 Upper Deck #469
Skylight   .40-$1

❏ '93 Upper Deck All-Star
Weekend #34 $2-4

❏ '93-94 Upper Deck
All-Rookies #AR1 $12-20

❏ '93-94 Upper Deck
European #4 All-Star $2.50-5

❏ '93-94 Upper Deck
European #35 All-Division $2.50-5

❏ '93-94 Upper Deck European
#69 Rookie Standouts $2.50-5

❏ '93-94 Upper Deck
European #220 $5-10

❏ '93-94 Upper Deck
Flight Team #FT16 $30-40

❏ '93-94 Upper Deck
Future Heroes #35 $12-20

❏ '93-94 Upper Deck
Holojams #H19 $2-4

❏ '93-94 Upper Deck
Locker Talk #LT3 $18-30

❏ '93-94 Upper Deck
ProView #102 3-D Jams   .40-$1

❏ '93-94 Upper Deck
ProView #32 $1-2

❏ '93-94 Upper Deck ProView #79
3-D Playground Legends   .40-$1

❏ '93-94 Upper Deck SE #32 $1-2

❏ '93-94 Upper Deck SE
Behind the Glass #G13 $7.50-15

❏ '93-94 Upper Deck SE
Die-Cut All-Stars #E13 $90-140

'93-94 SkyBox Shaq Talk #2

❏ '93-94 Upper Deck SE
Electric Court #32 $3-6

❏ '93-94 Upper Deck SE
Electric Gold #32 $50-100

❏ '93-94 Upper Deck SE
USA Trade #24 $4.50-9

❏ '93-94 Upper Deck Sheet
#6 Multiplayer $7.50-15

❏ '93-94 Upper Deck
Team MVPs #TM19 $2.50-5

❏ '93-94 Upper Deck
Wal-Mart Jumbos #LT3 $4-8

❏ '94 Classic Draft Picks #69
Centers of Attention   .08-.25

❏ '94 Classic Draft Picks

Chrome #NNO $15-25

❏ '94 Classic Draft Picks
Autograph #NNO $250-400

❏ '94 Classic Draft Picks Gold
#69 Centers of Attention   .50-$1

❏ '94 Classic Draft Picks
Printer's Proofs #69
Centers of Attention $6.50-$12.50

❏ '94 Classic Four-Sport
Shaq-Fu Tip Cards set* $12-20

❏ '94 Classic Ceramiques
5-card set $20-40

❏ '94 Classic Ceramiques
Artist's Proof 5-card set $250-300

❏ '94 Classic Images Sudden
Impact* #SI9   .40-$1

❏ '94 Classic Images* #128
Black and White   .10-.30

❏ '94 Classic Images*
#36 Rap   .10-.30

❏ '94 Flair USA
#'s 73-80 $1.25-2.50 each

❏ '94 SkyBox Blue Chips
#20 Multiplayer   .20-.50

❏ '94 SkyBox Blue Chips
#21 Multiplayer   .10-.20

❏ '94 SkyBox Blue Chips
#29 Multiplayer   .10-.20

❏ '94 SkyBox Blue Chips
#30 Multiplayer   .10-20

❏ '94 SkyBox Blue Chips
#39 Multiplayer   .10-.20

❏ '94 SkyBox Blue Chips
#40 Multiplayer   .15-30

❏ '94 SkyBox Blue Chips
#41 Multiplayer   .10-20

❏ '94 SkyBox Blue Chips
#42 Multiplayer   .10-.20

❏ '94 SkyBox Blue Chips
#44 Multiplayer   .15-.30

❏ '94 SkyBox Blue Chips #57   .25-.50

❏ '94 SkyBox Blue Chips
#66 Multiplayer   .10-.20

❏ '94 SkyBox Blue Chips
#70 Multiplayer   .10-.20

❏ '94 SkyBox Blue Chips
#71 Multiplayer   .10-.20

❏ '94 SkyBox Blue Chips
#72 Multiplayer   .15-.30

❏ '94 SkyBox Blue Chips
#73 Multiplayer   .15-.30

❏ '94 SkyBox Blue Chips
#75 Multiplayer   .15-.30

❏ '94 SkyBox Blue Chips
#77 Multiplayer   .15-.30

❏ '94 SkyBox Blue Chips
#79 Multiplayer   .15-.30

❏ '94 SkyBox Blue Chips
#81Multiplayer   .10-.20

❏ '94 SkyBox Blue Chips
#82 Multiplayer   .10-.20

❏ '94 SkyBox Blue Chips
#83 Multiplayer   .15-.30

❏ '94 SkyBox Blue Chips
#84 Multiplayer   .10-.20

❏ '94 SkyBox Blue Chips
#87   .15-.30

❏ '94 SkyBox Blue Chips
#88   .15-.30

❏ '94 SkyBox Blue Chips
Foil #F3 $6.50-12.50

- ❏ '94 SkyBox Blue Chips Foil #F4 $6.50-$12.50
- ❏ '94 SkyBox Blue Chips Foil #SP $6.50-12.50
- ❏ '94 SkyBox Blue Chips Prototypes #3 Multiplayer $2-4
- ❏ '94 Upper Deck USA #'s 49-54 .40-$1 Each
- ❏ '94 Upper Deck USA Chalk Talk #CT9 $35-60
- ❏ '94 Upper Deck USA Follow Your Dreams #10 Rebounds $6-10
- ❏ '94 Upper Deck USA Follow Your Dreams #10 Assists $6-10
- ❏ '94 Upper Deck USA Follow Your Dreams #10 Scoring $6-10
- ❏ '94 Upper Deck USA Follow Your Dreams #10 Rebound Exchange $6-10
- ❏ '94 Upper Deck USA Follow Your Dreams #10 Assist Exchange $6-10
- ❏ '94 Upper Deck USA Follow Your Dreams #10 Scoring Exchange $6-10
- ❏ '94 Upper Deck USA Gold Medal #'s 49-54 $1.25-2.50
- ❏ '94-95 Classic Assets* #26 .40-$1
- ❏ '94-95 Classic Assets Silver Signature* #26 $3-6
- ❏ '94-95 Classic Assets Calling Cards One Minute/$2* #17 $2.50-5
- ❏ '94-95 Classic Assets Calling Cards $25* #3 $50-80
- ❏ '94-95 Classic Assets Die-Cut* #DC1 $9-15
- ❏ '94-95 Collector's Choice #184 Tip-Off .20-.50
- ❏ '94-95 Collector's Choice #197 All-Star Advice .20-.50
- ❏ '94-95 Collector's Choice #205 NBA Profiles .20-.50
- ❏ '94-95 Collector's Choice #232 $.40-$1
- ❏ '94-95 Collector's Choice #390 Blueprint for Success .20-.50
- ❏ '94-95 Collector's Choice #400 World of Trivia .20-.50
- ❏ '94-95 Collector's Choice Crash the Game Rebounds #R10 $6-10
- ❏ '94-95 Collector's Choice Crash the Game Scoring #S7 $10-20
- ❏ '94-95 Collector's Choice Gold Signature #184 Tip-Off $25-50
- ❏ '94-95 Collector's Choice Gold Signature #197 All-Star Advice $25-50
- ❏ '94-95 Collector's Choice Gold Signature #205 NBA Profiles $25-50
- ❏ '94-95 Collector's Choice Gold Signature #232 $60-100
- ❏ '94-95 Collector's Choice Gold Signature #390 Blueprint for Success $25-50
- ❏ '94-95 Collector's Choice Gold Signature #400 World of Trivia $25-50
- ❏ '94-95 Collector's Choice Silver Signature #184 Tip-Off $1-2

- ❏ '94-95 Collector's Choice Silver Signature #197 All-Star Advice $1-2
- ❏ '94-95 Collector's Choice Silver Signature #205 NBA Profiles $1-2
- ❏ '94-95 Collector's Choice Silver Signature #232 $2-4
- ❏ '94-95 Collector's Choice Silver Signature #390 Blueprint for Success $1-2
- ❏ '94-95 Collector's Choice Silver Signature #400 World of Trivia $1-2
- ❏ '94-95 Finest #32 $6-12
- ❏ '94-95 Finest #280 Finest's Best $2.50-5
- ❏ '94-95 Finest Cornerstone #1 $30-50
- ❏ '94-95 Finest Iron Men #1 $30-50
- ❏ '94-95 Finest Lottery Prize #15 $15-25
- ❏ '94-95 Finest Refractor #32 $70-120
- ❏ '94-95 Finest Refractor #280 Finest's Best $30-60
- ❏ '94-95 Flair #107 $3-6
- ❏ '94-95 Flair #168 USA $1.50-3
- ❏ '94-95 Flair Center Spotlight #4 $30-50
- ❏ '94-95 Flair Hot Number #12 $9-15
- ❏ '94-95 Flair Rejectors #5 $30-50
- ❏ '94-95 Flair Scoring Power #5 $9-15
- ❏ '94-95 Fleer Promo Sheet #160 .75-1.50
- ❏ '94-95 Fleer #160 .40-$1
- ❏ '94-95 Fleer All-Stars #9 $4-8
- ❏ '94-95 Fleer League Leaders #5 $3-6
- ❏ '94-95 Fleer Team Leaders #7 Multiplayer .75-$2
- ❏ '94-95 Fleer Towers of Power #8 $7-12
- ❏ '94-95 Fleer Triple Threats #7 $1.50-3
- ❏ '94-95 Fleer Young Lions #5 $2.50-5
- ❏ '94-95 Hoops #152 .40-$1
- ❏ '94-95 Hoops #231 All-Star .20-.50
- ❏ '94-95 Hoops #256 League Leader Multiplayer .01-.05
- ❏ '94-95 Hoops #257 League Leader Multiplayer .01-.05
- ❏ '94-95 Hoops Big Numbers #BN5 $10-20
- ❏ '94-95 Hoops Big Numbers Rainbow #BN5 $7.50-15
- ❏ '94-95 Hoops Mail-Away 100-Card Press Sheet $15-25
- ❏ '94-95 Hoops Mail-Away 100-Card Press Sheet Autograph $250-500
- ❏ '94-95 Hoops Predators #P3 $2.50-5
- ❏ '94-95 Hoops Supreme Court #SC33 $2-4

- ❏ '94-95 Hoops Team Sheets #11 Multiplayer $2.50-5
- ❏ '94-95 Jam Session #136 $1-2.50
- ❏ '94-95 Jam Session Gamebreakers #6 $2.50-5
- ❏ '94-95 Jam Session Slam Dunk Heroes #7 $15-30
- ❏ '94 Jam Session Ticket Stubs #3 $5-10
- ❏ '94 Kenner Starting Lineup Club #1 $45-75
- ❏ '94-95 Kenner Starting Lineup #20 $10-20
- ❏ '94-95 SkyBox #118 $1-2
- ❏ '94-95 SkyBox #187 Dynamic Duals .30-.75
- ❏ '94-95 SkyBox Center Stage #CS2 $35-60
- ❏ '94-95 SkyBox Revolution #R6 $30-50
- ❏ '94-95 SkyBox Slammin' Universe #SU19 $2-4
- ❏ '94 SkyBox USA #'s 67-72 .40-$1 each
- ❏ '94 SkyBox USA Champion Gold #'s 67-72 $2.50-5 each

'94-95 Flair #107

- ❏ '94 SkyBox USA Dream Play #DP12 $18-30
- ❏ '94 SkyBox USA On the Court #14 $6-10
- ❏ '94 SkyBox USA Portraits #PT12 $75-120
- ❏ '92-93 Sports Illustrated for Kids II #341 $1.50-3
- ❏ '94-95 Stadium Club #32 $1-2
- ❏ '94-95 Stadium Club #102 College Teammates Multiplayer .20-.50
- ❏ '94-95 Stadium Club #355 Faces of the Game .40-$1
- ❏ '94-95 Stadium Club First Day Issue #32 $60-100
- ❏ '94-95 Stadium Club Beam Team #19 $18-30
- ❏ '94-95 Stadium Club Dynasty and Destiny #7B $1.50-3
- ❏ '94-95 Stadium Club First Day Issue #102 College Teammates Multiplayer $12.50-25

- ❏ '94-95 Stadium Club First Day Issue #355 Faces of the Game $25-50
- ❏ '94-95 Stadium Club Rising Stars #5 $20-35
- ❏ '94-95 Stadium Club Super Skills #22 $18-30
- ❏ '94-95 Stadium Club Super Teams #19 Multiplayer $18-30
- ❏ '94-95 Stadium Club Team of the Future #5 $15-25
- ❏ '94-95 Topps #13 All-Star .20-.50
- ❏ '94-95 Topps #100 Paint Patrol .20-.50
- ❏ '94-95 Topps #299 .40-$1
- ❏ '94-95 Topps #300 From the Roof .20-.50
- ❏ '94-95 Topps Spectralight #13 All-Star $3-6
- ❏ '94-95 Topps Spectralight #100 Paint Patrol $3-6
- ❏ '94-95 Topps Spectralight #299 $6-12
- ❏ '94-95 Topps Spectralight #300 From the Roof $3-6
- ❏ '94-95 Topps Franchise/ Futures #17 $12-20
- ❏ '94-95 Topps Own the Game #28 Rebounds $4-8
- ❏ '94-95 Topps Own the Game #29 Scoring $5-10
- ❏ '94-95 Topps Own the Game #30 Swats $4-8
- ❏ '94-95 Ultra #135 $1-2
- ❏ '94-95 Ultra All-NBA #12 $3-6
- ❏ '94-95 Ultra Jam City #8 $12-20
- ❏ '94-95 Ultra Rebound Kings #7 $1.50-3
- ❏ '94-95 Ultra Scoring Kings #5 $28-45
- ❏ '94-95 Ultra Power #8 $3-6
- ❏ '94-95 Ultra Power in the Key #7 $5-10
- ❏ '94-95 Upper Deck #100 $1-2
- ❏ '94-95 Upper Deck #178 USA .40-$1
- ❏ '94-95 Upper Deck #23 All-NBA Team .40-$1
- ❏ '94-95 Upper Deck Predictors Award Winners #H21 MVP $12-20
- ❏ '94-95 Upper Deck Predictors Award Winners #H3 All-Star MVP $9-15
- ❏ '94-95 Upper Deck Predictors League Leaders #R2 Scorers $12-20
- ❏ '94-95 Upper Deck Predictors League Leaders #R21 Rebounds $9-15
- ❏ '94-95 Upper Deck Predictors League Leaders #R35 Blocks $9-15
- ❏ '94-95 Upper Deck Slam Dunk Stars #S12 $25-40
- ❏ '94-95 Upper Deck Special Edition #SE152 $2.50-5
- ❏ '94-95 Upper Deck Special Edition Gold #SE152 $30-60
- ❏ '94-95 Upper Deck Promo Sheets Series 2 #1Multiplayer $3

cards from multisport set

STORY BY JACK DEVRIES

PENCILS BY AL BIGLEY

INKS BY DAN PIRARO

COLOR BY JOHN MARSHALL
AND OMAR MEDIANO

LETTERING BY JOHN MARSHALL
AND OMAR MEDIANO

STORY CONSULTANTS:
PEPPER HASTINGS,
JAY JOHNSON AND
RUDY KLANCNIK

EDITOR: FRED L. REED III

LIVIN' LARGE

RRRRRIIIIIINNNNGGGGGG

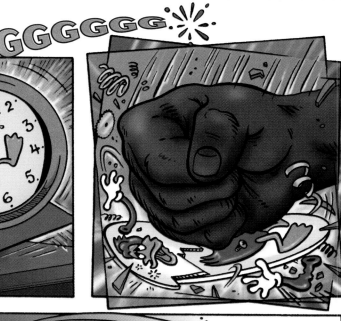

A DAY IN THE LIFE FOR SHAQUILLE O'NEAL STARTS OFF NORMALLY . . .

I'M ALWAYS TIRED THE DAY AFTER PLAYING THE HORNETS . . . HAVE TO POUND ON 'EM SO MUCH. OH WELL, GOT THE KNICKS TONIGHT.

SMAK!

RIP!

NOT *AGAIN!*

LOOKS LIKE ANOTHER DAY'S WORK FOR THE CARPENTER.

JUST GETTING THE NEWSPAPER CAN BE HAZARDOUS TO MY HOUSE!

THE NBA'S NEWEST SUPERSTAR LIKES TO BEGIN HIS DAY WITH A NICE, HOT SHOWER . . .

OK, BRO, I'M SET TO GO IN.

GET READY BOYS, HE'S GOING IN!

WE'RE ALL SET HERE, MR. O'NEAL. ENJOY YOUR SHOWER.

FINALLY GOT MY OWN RESERVOIR. NOW EVERYBODY IN ORLANDO WILL STOP SAYING, 'SHAQ USED UP ALL THE HOT WATER!'

MAN, ALONZO'S GOT A HARD HEAD. GOT ME A LITTLE BRUISE ON MY ELBOW.

BESIDES TONIGHT'S GAME, SHAQUILLE HAS A BUSY SCHEDULE TO ATTEND TO . . .

LET'S SEE, GOTTA FILM THE COMMERCIAL, STOP BY THE RECORDING STUDIO, PRACTICE SOME FOUL SHOTS . . .

SHAZAM, IT'S TIME FOR YOU TO GET UP, TOO!

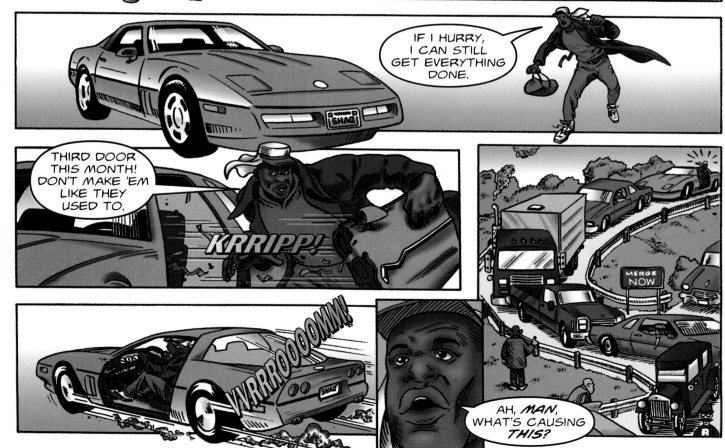

Superstar
Gallery

it's

a good thing Shaquille O'Neal stands 7-1, tips the scales at more than 300 pounds and eats fiberglass backboards for breakfast. Carrying the weight of an entire hobby isn't for the meek.

Since bursting onto the professional scene just a year and a half ago, Shaq has meant as much to the sports card hobby as Magic and Bird meant to the NBA. The excitement O'Neal's NBA entrance created was the perfect remedy for a hobby starting to experience some troubling symptoms.

Beckett Focus on Future Stars®, our monthly multisport magazine, put a full-court press on Shaq when he was destroying basket supports and opponents at LSU.

Beckett Basketball Monthly was so pumped up over Shaq's first real job, we helped him on with his new work clothes. On the front cover of issue #27 (October 1992), thanks to some fancy computer footwork, O'Neal appears in the heat of battle wearing a Magic jersey. Since he didn't start his rookie campaign until November, and he chose No. 32 instead of his college No. 33, readers got a captivating sneak preview and a one-of-a-kind keepsake.

But that was just the start of the fun. Shaq and *Beckett*® have become great teammates in the last 2-1/2 years. And there seems to be no end in sight. •

when *Beckett Focus on Future Stars*® turned 25 (issues, that is) in May 1993, Shaq helped us celebrate as the subject of special cover artwork.

beckett

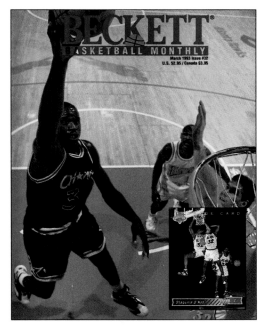

readers discovered what a backboard sees the millisecond before the Shaq Attack thunders home another rim-rattling jam on issue #32 (*Beckett Basketball Monthly*, March 1993).

shaq muscled his way to Rookie of the Year honors and pumped new life into a position many fans had forgotten (*Beckett Basketball Monthly* issue #31, February 1993).

remembers

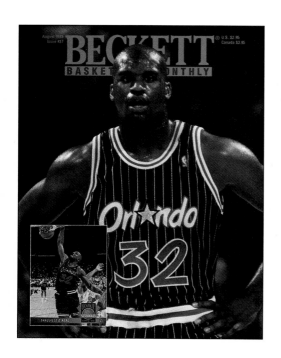

shaq is so big . . . How big is he? He's so big *Beckett Basketball Monthly* (issue #37, August 1993) needed both of its covers to show off this massive talent. Inside, readers found the collection they had been dreaming about.

the uniform may have changed since *Future Stars* issue #8 (December 1991), but the dunks remain the same — awesome!

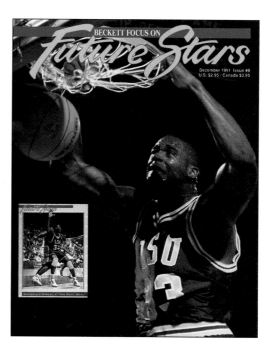

predicting the future was a piece of cake with O'Neal. Even before Shaq played a college game, pro scouts were lining up to catch a glimpse of this skyscraper. Our story in *Future Stars* issue #2 (June 1991) detailed his rapid rise to stardom and revealed one of his special tutors — Hall of Fame center Kareem Abdul-Jabbar.

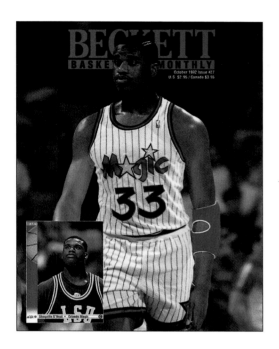

what do you get when you mix Shaq with a former NBA bench warmer? A cover to remember, that's what. Using Terry Catledge's torso and, of course, uniform, *Beckett Basketball Monthly* (issue #27, October 1992) gave fans what they wanted: Shaq in a Magic uniform before he tipped off for his maiden pro season.

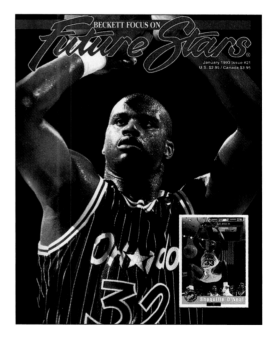

the only chink in this youngster's armor was his free-throw shooting. But his form doesn't look too shabby on *Future Stars* issue #21 (January 1993).

shaq's cinematic debut in *Blue Chips* was pictured in the pages of *Beckett Basketball Monthly* issue #44 (March 1994).

shaq's most recent appearance on a *BKM* cover, in April 1995 (issue #57), and the accompanying "Closer Look" focused on Shaq's determination to get even better — a frightening possibility for opponents.

owing to Shaq's swelling popularity throughout the course of his rookie NBA season, we devoted an entire issue to him by making him the subject of our fourth *Beckett Tribute* in 1993.

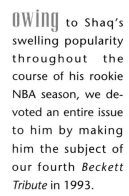

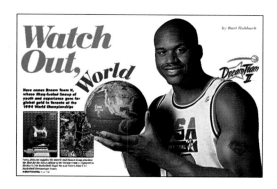

shaq was pictured with four of his Dream Team II teammates on the cover of *Beckett Basketball Monthly* issue #49 (August 1994). As the results showed, the world had plenty to be wary of.

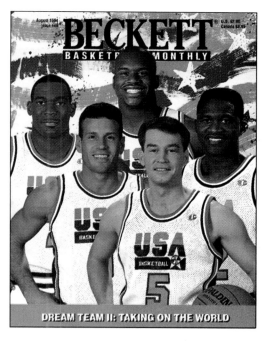

DREAM TEAM II: TAKING ON THE WORLD

who more fitting to feature on the cover of the 50th issue of *Beckett Basketball Monthly* (September 1994) than Shaq? Tom Fleming's artwork captured Shaq at his fearsome best.

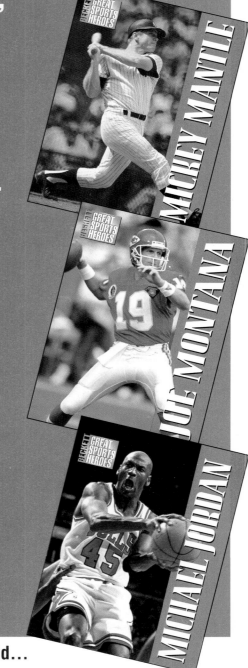